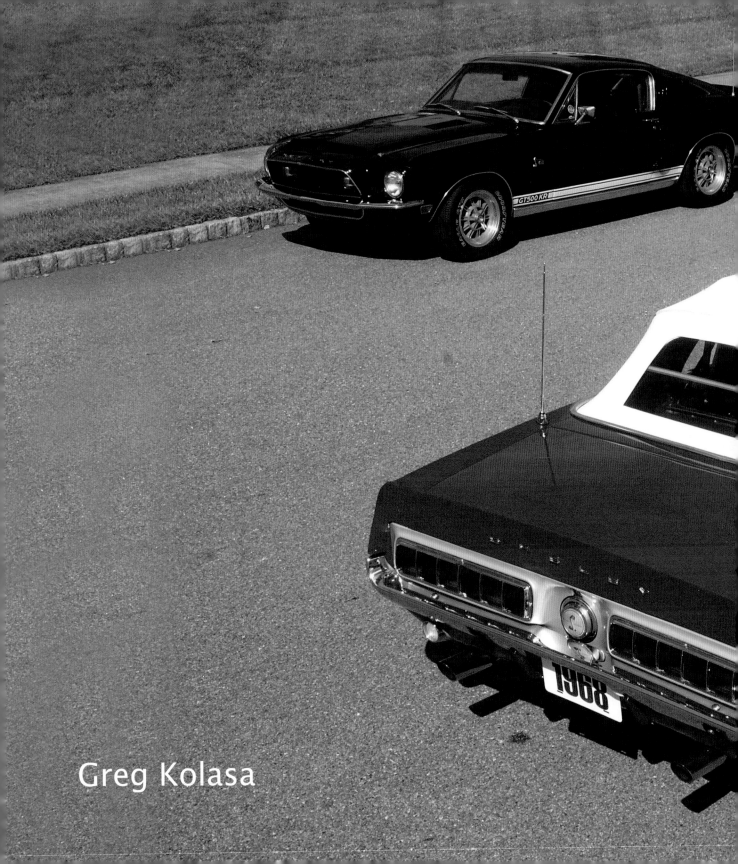

Greg Kolasa

1968 Shelby MUSTANG
GT350, GT500 AND GT500 KR

CarTech®

CarTech®

CarTech®, Inc.
838 Lake Street South
Forest Lake, MN 55025
Phone: 651-277-1200 or 800-551-4754
Fax: 651-277-1203
cartechbooks.com

Edit by Bob Wilson
Layout by Connie DeFlorin

ISBN 978-1-61325-292-5
Item No. CT572

Library of Congress Cataloging-in-Publication Data

Names: Kolasa, Greg, author.
Title: 1968 Shelby GT350, GT500 & GT500 KR : in detail / Greg Kolasa.
Description: Forest Lake, MN : CarTech, [2017]
Identifiers: LCCN 2016010603 | ISBN 9781613252925
Subjects: LCSH: Shelby automobile. | Cobra automobile. | Mustang automobile.
 | Shelby, Carroll, 1923-2012.
Classification: LCC TL215.S48 .K65 2017 | DDC 629.222/2--dc23
LC record available at https://lccn.loc.gov/2016010603

Written, edited, and designed in the U.S.A.
Printed in China
10 9 8 7 6 5 4 3 2 1

Front Cover: The 1968 Shelby model year was notable for five, three-car groups of big- and small-block fastbacks done in special colors. One of those fastback trios was painted a bright orange color that, just a year later, made it into Ford's new-car brochures as Calypso Coral; Mercury called it Competition Orange. (Photo Courtesy Pete Disher)

Frontispiece:
The 1968 model year saw the return to two headlights. An introductory press release described the new illumination scheme: "In addition to the new front end styling, single 7¼-inch double-filament sealed-beam lights have been fitted and are complemented by separately circuited rectangular driving lights mounted inside the oval grill [sic] opening."

Title Page:
Perhaps the biggest news for 1968 was the availability of both the GT350 and GT500 in the Model 76 (convertible) body style, complementing the existing Model 63 fastback. Tried experimentally a couple of years earlier, the ragtop Shelby proved to be very popular. Nearly 3 out of every 10 '68 cars built had soft tops.

Contents Page:
The second time's a charm. Tried in 1965 as an unsuccessful styling experiment for the '66 Shelby, fitting '65 T-Bird taillights worked better on the '68 Shelby (which had a rear panel designed especially to accept the 'Bird lamps). A silver tail panel and chrome "S-H-E-L-B-Y" lettering added visual interest to the too-simple '67 Shelby transom. (Photo Courtesy LegendaryMotorCar.com)

DISTRIBUTION BY:

Europe
PGUK
63 Hatton Garden
London EC1N 8LE, England
Phone: 020 7061 1980 • Fax: 020 7242 3725
pguk.co.uk

Australia
Renniks Publications Ltd.
3/37-39 Green Street
Banksmeadow, NSW 2109, Australia
Phone: 2 9695 7055 • Fax: 2 9695 7355
renniks.com

TABLE OF CONTENTS

ACKNOWLEDGMENTS

Whether you are a supporter or detractor of Carroll Shelby, you have to concede that his management philosophy of surrounding himself with the best, brightest, and most talented people to accomplish an objective, worked. That's the approach I followed in creating this book. Although the appropriateness of using Shelby's technique to write a book about his cars is certainly apparent, the real reason I followed that model was because it works. There is some degree of lunacy to penning any work on Shelby's Mustangs without tapping into the vast resources of the Shelby American Automobile Club (SAAC) and its registrars and concours judges, so I took full advantage of their willingness to share their collective expertise. Rodney Harrold, Dave Mathews, Howard Pardee, Pete Disher, Jeff Speegle, and SAAC founder and National Director, Rick Kopec (who also shares more than a little of the blame for launching my literary career, if I dare call it that) took it as their personal challenge to make me sound as if I know what I am talking about; I am thankful for their success.

While I can claim responsibility for some for the photos of the Shelbys, Mustangs, and other Fords that appear between these covers, others are the work of the car owners, some of whom went far above and beyond to provide superb images of the wonderful machines (many of them driven regularly) of which they are caretakers. Sincere thanks to

Dennis Blocker (CSX 3311), Tim Brillhart (8T02R206064-02591), Dominic Ciliberto and Diana Duffee (8T03S115994-00136, 8T02J188441-02993, and S.F.M. 6S2050), Tom Clark (1968 Mustang GT California Special), Colin Comer (8T02J205264-03218), Tony Conover (8T02R205374-03447), Rich DiMarino (1968 Mustang GT California Special), Pete Disher (8T02R204798-03206), Lee Dixon (8T02S129547-00555), Scott Fuller (8T03S185133-02837, 8T02R205375-03447, and 8T03R216160-04391), Bev Harrold (1968 Mustang GT California Special), Rodney Harrold (8T02R201713-02267), Bill Hartmann (1964-1/2 Mustang Hardtop), Dan Hayenhjelm (1961 Ford Falcon), Mike Hudock (8T02R210376-03760), Martin Jackler (67200F3-0069), Peter Larkin (S.F.M. 6S327), Charlie McHose (8T03S134540-00987), David and Kellie Meador (8T02S143434-01561), Gary and Deb Miller (8T02J126809-00397), Gary and Jason Miller (1967 Shelby "Little Red" replica), Paul M. Newitt (1968 Mustang GT California Special), Scott Nickett (1962 Ford Thunderbird 09KR0166), Carol Padden (S.F.M. 6S1012), Howard Pardee (S.F.M. 5R095), Linda and Len Perham (S.F.M. 6S2377), Robert Perruso (8T02J193184-02085), Richard Pozarycki (8T02J192467-02184), Bill and Cyndi Prohidney (07H0318), David Russell (67400F8U00723), Simeone Foundation Automotive Museum (CSX 2287 and XGT-1) Scott Smith (8T02J134489-00930), Jan Sochurek (S.F.M. 5S392),

Mike Tillery (8T02R205338-03382), Lance Tarnutzer (8T03R2210094-03473), Samuel Vassallo (8T03S149444-01445 and 8T02R216177-04408), Brian Walshe ('66 Mustang GT "K" fastback), Fred Warf (8T02J204810-03271),and Jim Wojcik (8T02R210136-03515).

Kevin Marti of Marti Autoworks (marti-auto.com) provided valuable assistance in decoding VIN and ID tags and determining various cars' build dates; Marty Jackler willingly shared his vast knowledge of Ford parts and their applications (past and present); and Scott Fuller of Scott Fuller Reproductions (sfreproductions.com) supplied more information than I ever knew even existed on the many unique aspects of the '68 Shelbys and High Country Special Mustangs. Jerry Heasley and the good folks up north at Legendary Motor-Car Company (legendarymotorcar.com) happily shared their spectacular images of the prototype 1968 GT500s and Bob Wilson pitched in by neatly filling a photographic void that developed in Chapter 4. Perhaps nobody knows more about the California and High Country Special Mustangs than Paul M. Newitt; his tutelage on the subject was invaluable and equally appreciated. Frank Costanzo, Mike Deliberto, and Rich DiMarino of the Garden State Region Mustang Club generously offered their assistance in tracking down the owners of some of these "almost Shelby" notchbacks.

As I sat down to condense all of this information into (hopefully) coherent text, Carol Padden proofread my multiple attempts at each chapter. And speaking of chapters, since a complete itemization of the assistance provided by Lowell Otter and J. D. Kaltenbach would fill a separate one, I will simply, but most sincerely, say "thank you" to them, to all the other generous folks, and to anyone I have thoughtlessly omitted. Their assistance made this book what it is and I am grateful.

Having a file cabinet full of factory documents for reference is great but it is only partially complete without the personal anecdotes and experiences (think of them as explanatory footnotes) of people who were there "back in the day." A very big "thanks" is due to GT350 Project Engineer Chuck Cantwell; Ford stylist Charlie McHose; SAAC Registrar (and original '68 Shelby owner) Vincent Liska; and ACSCO Products President Tom McIntyre, for telling their tales of how things really went down.

And finally, I know that I can speak for Shelby enthusiasts everywhere when I say that we are appreciative beyond words to Jack Redeker for not only so generously sharing some of his wonderful period images but even more so for not heeding the "no photography allowed" admonitions given during his 1968 A. O. Smith factory tour in the first place.

CHAPTER 1

UNDERSTANDING CARROLL SHELBY'S MUSTANGS

When the Mustang debuted in April 1964, it wasn't an overnight success. It didn't take anywhere near that long; it was instantaneous. The car was sleek, shapely, sexy, spiffy, snappy, snazzy, and certainly sporty, but it wasn't a sports car, and that's what Ford needed. Carroll Shelby soon fixed that. (Photo Courtesy Bill Hartmann)

To fully appreciate and understand the 1968 Shelby Mustangs, a brief history of the Mustang, the Ford Motor Company, and the state of automotive affairs in the United States in the late 1940s through the early 1960s is a prerequisite. When the 1965 Mustang debuted at the New York World's Fair on April 17, 1964, to say that the car was an instant smash hit is an understatement of epic proportions.

The Mustang's effect on not only Detroit, but on popular American culture, in general, was nothing short of profound. Compared to Ford's then-current (and more than just a little bit stuffy and stodgy) stable, the pert little coupe was not only a

styling coup, but it also begat an entirely new class of automobile: the not-coincidentally-named "pony car" class. While Ford basked very publicly in the glow of its recent achievement, privately it lamented the one nagging criticism of the Mustang. Despite the car's drop-dead good looks, its unprecedented bang-for-the-buck value, its arm's-length options list, and its sizzling performance, Ford couldn't overcome the fact that although the Mustang was no doubt a *sporty* car, it wasn't a *sports* car. Ford just didn't *want* a sports car; it *needed* a sports car.

Ford had kicked off its decade-long "Total Performance" marketing program

Myriad options do not a sports car make. Adding every available performance extra to a base Mustang (High Performance 289, 4-speed transmission, disc brakes, GT suspension) put the car very close to, and in fact, even formed the basis for, a sports car, but it wasn't quite there. Shelby American moved the ball across the goal line.

the year before Mustang's debut. Chevrolet had had a sports car for almost 10 years. Ford's performance program, identified by just two brief words, was itself the product of V-J Day. It was the beginning of the automotive performance movement in the United States.

PEACE, PROSPERITY AND PERFORMANCE

It is not a stretch at all to say that the need for the Mustang to be recognized as a sports car really began at the end of World War II. With the end of hostilities,

Ford had numerous reasons for needing its new Mustang to be recognized as a sports car. The company needed a sports car to fit into its new Total Performance marketing and motorsports campaign. It also needed to counter the Corvette, which, by the time Total Performance was up and running, had already marked a decade of as Chevrolet proudly proclaimed it, "America's Sports Car."

In 1960, Ford debuted the stodgy, lackluster, but altogether practical, Falcon. Ironically, that sedate little sedan led the way for Ford's entry into motorsports. Powered by hand-built, high-performance 260s, the Holman-Moody–prepared Falcon Sprints didn't win the 1963 Monte Carlo Rally outright, but it fired a warning shot across the bow of international motorsports and served notice that the Blue Oval was a force to be reckoned with.

a massive influx of millions of ex-serviceman, many of them barely post-teenage, flooded back into the United States, and back into civilian life. During the late 1940s and early 1950s, the hot rod movement went pedal-to-the-metal as ex-GIs sought to fulfill their need for speed. They formed the consumer base that purchased huge numbers of automobiles, and their offspring formed the heart of the American car-buying public for the next generation. Everything automotive in the post-war United States was centered on two important attributes: speed and performance. Buyers couldn't get enough of either, and Detroit was only too happy to oblige. Cars became faster, more powerful, and more exciting with each model year. Everyone's, that is, except Ford's.

In the midst of all this speed and performance, Ford was, automotively speaking, still in the dark ages. By the early 1950s, when General Motors had introduced the Corvette, Ford continued to hold onto the reputation of creating cars that would satisfy most new car buyers' grandfathers. Ford's product

lineup was, very simply put, not very exciting, and that was no accident; it was by design. Under the leadership of Robert McNamara, Ford continued to develop and produce logical, sensible, fiscally responsible, but altogether unexciting automobiles.

That changed in 1960 when John F. Kennedy was elected president. That event in Washington had far-reaching implications for the future of the Ford Motor Company, all driven by the power vacuum created at the highest levels of Dearborn management by the President-elect. It started when he tapped McNamara to be his Secretary of Defense.

That left a hole at the top, which was filled by Henry Ford II. That, in turn, left various openings at levels just below him. One of them was the vacancy of president of the Ford Division. It was filled by someone considered by most insiders (and certainly those corporate ladder-climbers vying for occupancy of the president's office) to be an unlikely candidate: Lee Iacocca. With leadership of the division and Henry II's ear, Iacocca was one of the few Ford leaders who truly understood the effect the Baby Boom would have on car buying. He recognized that by the early 1960s, the United States had more young people than at any other time in the country's history and that this equated to the country having more young car buyers than at any other time. And every one of them craved speed and performance.

Slowly at first, then with the ever-increasing speed of a snowball down a mountain, the rest of Ford management began to grasp that they could use speed and performance to their advantage. Potential car buyers (even those not necessarily interested in speed and performance) concluded that because of Ford's motorsports victories, its products must be superior to those of the other manufacturers.

In the spring of 1962, Ford officially withdrew from the 1958 Resolution on Speed and Advertising (the so-called, self-imposed "Performance Ban," instituted by the automobile manufacturers themselves, ostensibly in the interest of safety). This stated that Ford (and not another organization, even one of which Ford was a member) should determine what course its company should follow in the context of automotive safety. When asked if withdrawal from the ban meant that Ford was once again going to dip its toe into the motorsports pool, new president Henry Ford II answered that they were not merely going to dip a toe, but that they were "going in with both feet."

The summer of 1963 saw Ford launch the largest, most extensive, expansive (and likely expensive) motorsports program in the history of the American automobile.

WIN ON SUNDAY, SELL ON MONDAY

The program was known as "Total Performance" and its scope was equaled only by its expenditures. Although the best-known aspect of Total Performance was the nearly decade-long motorsports program, Total Performance was actually an overarching marketing philosophy, in the context that car buyers, after examination of a Ford car's *total performance*, decided that the Ford product was clearly superior. The objective of the motorsports program was elegantly (and also expensively) simple: to dominate *all* forms of motorsports, drag racing, stock car racing, sports car racing, IndyCar racing, or any other kind of racing. If it was racing, Ford wanted to dominate it, and cost didn't matter.

The subtitle of Total Performance, "improving the breed through open competition," was intended to thwart criticism that Ford's reemergence into performance was anti-safety. Because of what it was intended to achieve and the way it was to do so, Total Performance became known as the "Win on Sunday, Sell on Monday" sales philosophy.

The overall objective of the Total Performance motorsports program is often misunderstood, however. Ford's goal was to become the dominant force in motorsports, but that wasn't the end. It was the means to the end. The real end, very much counterintuitively, was increased sales to American car buyers of beige sedans and wood-on-the-side station wagons.

DECLARATION DENIED

Ford's lack of a real sports car in its product lineup could be resolved very easily if the new Mustang were recognized as a true sports car. To achieve that goal, Ford approached the one organization with the credentials and credibility to make that proclamation: the Sports Car Club of America (SCCA), which served as the sanctioning body for all amateur road racing in the United States. However, the company's plan of simply applying pressure to the SCCA to receive the all-important sports car declaration for Mustang was, amazingly to Ford, met with staunch refusal. The SCCA was fiercely independent and beholden to no one, not even a massive and powerful entity such as the Ford Motor Company. Instead of pressing the SCCA even harder, Ford realized that it would be easier to catch flies with Texas honey than with Dearborn vinegar. Ford turned to Carroll Shelby.

FROM "SECRETARY'S CAR" TO SPORTS CAR

When Lee Iacocca approached Carroll Shelby about making the Mustang a sports car, Shelby was somewhat reluctant to take on the project, feeling that the project would be a major distraction from his racing programs. Because of Ford's advertising that proclaimed the car's low price and fuel economy made it affordable, even for a secretary, he derided the Mustang as "a secretary's car." Shelby retold the story numerous times. He was far less than enthusiastic about Ford's "request," but he also saw the writing on the wall. In the beginning, the Cobra was the only race car in Ford's stable, and Shelby American was the benefactor of Ford's seemingly infinite corporate bank accounts.

However, with the advent of the GT40 and other in-house efforts, Ford put less and less emphasis on (and money into) Shelby's Cobras in favor of those other programs. Ford funding of Shelby's Cobras wasn't infinite; it definitely had an end, and Shelby knew that the end was approaching. In part because of that, and also

When the Ford GT40 appeared on the scene, Carroll Shelby knew that Ford's funding of his "powered by Ford" Cobras was no longer an infinite deal. He saw the Mustang GT350 project as additional revenue for a few more years, even if he didn't personally care to undertake the project. It turned out to be a fiscally wise decision and it made his good (and very powerful) Ford friend, Lee Iacocca, happy.

because the request had come from his now good friend Lee Iacocca (who, more than anyone else at Ford, was responsible for securing Ford funding for his Cobra project), Shelby agreed to take on the "secretary's car" project.

Shelby used Ford's steamrolling approach as a blueprint of what *not* to do when he called on John Bishop, who was both the director of the SCCA and a friend. Bishop laid out what Shelby needed to do to produce a Mustang sports car. It would have to be eligible for competition in one of SCCA's production sports car classes. These were delineated by the cars' performance potential to ensure relatively equal car-to-car competition. The car had to shed two seats because sports cars were two-seaters, and 100 examples needed to be produced by January of the year in which the car was to compete (in this case, 1965). Given that it was now already late summer of 1964, time was not an abundant community.

The production quantity minimum initially caused some consternation. Shelby American's experience with sales of the competition Cobras indicated that the requirement of 100 racers was nearly twice as many cars as there were potential customers. Thankfully, there was also relief in the regulations: all production cars were allowed a series of general deviations from the production version of the vehicle for the sake of performance, as well as for safety. In addition to these general modifications, the SCCA allowed a specific set of modifications, more limited in scope and number that had to be submitted and accepted beforehand by the SCCA in a

process known as "homologation." Specific modifications for racing went further still and were made over and above the general spec.

Although it may sound confusing, in the simplest of terms, there could effectively be two versions of Shelby's sports car version of the Mustang, the GT350: one for racing and one for street use. Both counted toward the 100-car production total.

GT350S FOR ROAD AND TRACK

Development of the Mustang into a race car was the primary emphasis of the new GT350 program, but there was also the secondary task to produce a street version, slightly detuned and only minimally more refined to satisfy production quantity minimums. The car took a somewhat convoluted route to become a sports car that was a bit different from that of other sports cars participating in SCCA competition.

You didn't have to lay out big bucks for a turnkey GT350 competition version to go racing. The similarity of the street version to its full-race brethren meant that, with minimal modifications (and hence, cash outlay), any street GT350 could be made into a race car. This approach had been undertaken by several owners who campaigned their (former) street machines very successfully on the strip as well as the track.

Objective achieved, with honors; the acceptance of the Mustang GT350 for competition in SCCA's B-Production racing class earned the Mustang the title of "sports car." Grabbing the national title three years in a row was the icing on that cake.

Normally, production sports cars were developed to satisfy a consumer demand for such a vehicle; in other words, to sell cars to the public for use on the street. After the cars had landed on the showroom floors, the nationwide performance craze of 1960s America almost demanded that there be a performance and ultimately a competition version of those cars. Therefore, efforts were undertaken to turn the street cars into race cars. The process for the Mustang GT350 was somewhat different.

When it was decided that a sports car version of the Mustang was needed, work began on a model that could be used on the track, which allowed the Mustang to legitimately lay claim to the title of "sports car." This was followed by the creation of a street brother. The unique GT350 process entailed a three-step process: street car (Ford Mustang) to race car (Shelby Ford Mustang GT350 competition model), then into another street car (Shelby Ford Mustang GT350 street version).

When Bishop and the SCCA visited Shelby American early in 1965 for their inspection, they found that the 100-car-production requirement was a bit short of fulfillment: only two race cars and a dozen or so street cars were complete. But the back lot behind Shelby's facility was filled to overflowing with more than 100 white Mustang fastbacks in various stages of transformation into GT350s. That indicated that Shelby was serious about meeting his production commitment.

Seeing Shelby's efforts, the Mustang GT350 was accepted for competition in SCCA's B-Production racing class for 1965. Ford's Mustang, or at least, one version of it, was now officially a sports car.

The newly minted race car showed what *kind* of sports car it was less than a month later when the GT350 won its first B-Production competition event. That winning trend continued for the remainder of the year. It culminated with Shelby American's Mustang GT350 being crowned as the 1965 SCCA B-Production National Champion sports car, a feat that it repeated in 1966 and 1967.

A SEDAN RACER NO LONGER

Shelby's people were not the first to put a Mustang on a racetrack. As soon as the Mustang was available for sale (in fact, even a little before), the little notchbacks hit all kinds of tracks in all levels of amateur and professional preparation where they quickly established themselves as worthy competitors. But they did so as sedan racers, not sports cars.

Shelby American changed that in a development process that began in late summer of 1964, when Ken Miles and Phil Remington began testing a pair of notchback Mustangs supplied by Ford. The fastback version of the Mustang, on which the GT350 was ultimately based, was still a couple of months away. They determined the exact modifications needed to improve the newborn pony's performance, based on testing and development performed by Ford engineers well before the cars arrived at Shelby American.

From these tests, plus what was learned from earlier Mustang race cars, came features that have become synonymous with the GT350: the lowered front suspension upper A-arms, the cross-engine-compartment Monte Carlo Bar, the Fairlane station wagon's large rear brake drums, and the aluminum high-rise intake topped with a Holley 715 cfm carburetor, to name a few. Simultaneously, Ford and Shelby American, along with the San Jose assembly plant, began discussing what could be added to and left off the Mustangs as they made their way down the assembly line, bound for Shelby American, and transformation into sports cars.

THE PROCESS EXPLAINED

In October 1964, Charles "Chuck" Cantwell left General Motors when he heard of a small automobile manufacturer in Los Angeles who was building race cars. Cantwell's first assignment with Shelby American was as the GT350's new project engineer and his first order of business was to learn the new pony car inside and out. For two weeks, he worked with (and at) Ford in Dearborn. He laid out long, detailed, hand-written spreadsheets of components and their functions, planning ways to improve the Mustang's performance.

Cantwell then toured the San Jose assembly line, picking out parts from the Ford production parts lineup to fulfill the Miles-Remington-Ford objectives. These items could be added relatively easily to,

Mustangs hit the racetracks in the United States, Europe, and Australia almost as soon as the car was available for sale. The little notchbacks quickly established themselves as worthy adversaries. Although they were winners, they won as sedans and that didn't allow Ford to lay claim to the Mustang as a sports car.

There was no "default" configuration to which Ford built Mustangs in the absence of a special order. Every pony (and in fact, every Ford product) was specifically designed in the configuration in which it was built. From a basic, no-option 6-cylinder coupe to a fully optioned HiPo GT convertible (and everything in between), every Mustang was a special order. Cars of similar characteristics, within a given sales district, formed a District Sales Order (DSO) that could be for a single car or several hundred identically equipped cars.

and deleted just as easily from, the Mustangs as they made their way down the San Jose line. That planning ensured that the Mustangs bound for Shelby American were built in the closest configuration as possible to the final product.

It has been a long-held belief that Ford churned out Mustangs by the train-carload, and every so often, one of them that met Shelby American's requirements for transformation into a GT350 was hastily spirited away by Shelby's fabricators. However, Shelby's Mustangs were actually carefully and precisely built for just that purpose based on a very specific set of predetermined requirements.

SPECIAL ORDERS

There was nothing random about the configuration of the Mustangs shipped to Shelby American for conversion to GT350s. And Ford did not randomly churn out regular production Mustangs by the thousands to be shipped to its dealers. Every Mustang and, in fact, every automobile that rolled out of a Ford assembly plant, was specially ordered the way it was eventually built.

The term "special order" almost always brings to mind exotic combinations of wild, high-performance options. In reality, every car was a special order, whether it was a four-door bench-seat sedan or one of the Blue Oval's latest and hottest Total Performance offerings. Every car scheduled for production was ordered by someone (an individual or a dealer) and no car was built unless there was a predetermined customer who specified how that car should be built. Likewise, there was no default configuration to which cars were built in the absence of a firm order; every car was a special order.

To keep track of its vehicle production, Ford divided the country into a series of about 40 areas, called districts. As each individual order for a car was placed by a dealer within a given district, the cars were grouped for production, by characteristics, in a District Special Order (DSO). The number of cars built within a single DSO was determined by the mechanical commonality of the car(s) requested. If no other vehicle with like qualities was ordered within that same district, that car was built under its own unique DSO. (Somewhat confusingly, "DSO" refers to both the special order for the car as well as the actual batch of cars built with carbon-copy attributes.)

If, however, multiple cars with identical traits (such as hundreds of kindred Mustangs, all destined for Shelby American) were ordered, that DSO contained multiple cars. Shelby submitted DSOs for cars to be built to a very specific configuration. These were processed and filled by Ford, just as for any Ford dealer in any district across the United States.

Shelby Mustangs were like no other muscle or performance car of the period. That's not a subjective evaluation based on the cars' relative "coolness" (or perhaps, in terms of performance, "hotness"). It's an objective assessment based on the car's unique construction method, designed from the beginning with very specific features for the conversion from

production sporty cars for the many to specialty sports cars for the few.

The GT350 also contributed to another almost revolutionary aspect of the Mustang. Just as the Model T defined an entirely new class of automobile (affordable, basic transportation for everyone), the Mustang was the first of a new category of car. Before long, cars including Chevrolet's Camaro, Plymouth's re-designed Barracuda, and Pontiac's Firebird (pony cars all) were developed in response to the new market created by Ford's Mustang.

Although the Ford Mustang defined a new class of automobile, in Shelby form, it also redefined the muscle car. Prior to the arrival of the GT350, muscle cars were large cars, such as the Chevrolet Impala and Pontiac GTO, powered by large engines. The Mustang GT350 took a pony car and gave it true performance potential; it made the pony car Mustang a contender in the muscle car arena. The two different classes of automobile, the pony car and the muscle car, converged in one package. From that point on, muscle cars were never the same again.

Whether production occurred in Southern California or Michigan, prior to each year's production, Ford determined the configuration of the platform Mustangs to be shipped to Shelby. Receiving those Mustangs in multiple DSOs, or batches, allowed for subtle "tweaks" to be incorporated into each successive group of cars and also relieved Shelby from having to purchase and find storage space for an entire year's worth of Mustangs at one time. Mustangs destined for GT350/GT500 conversion were so annotated on their individual build sheets. (Photo Courtesy Jack Redeker)

Although the '65 Mustang GT350's performance was by no means understated, the car's appearance was. It really didn't look like anything other than just a plain Mustang with stripes. Performance enthusiasts happily overlooked the visual shortcomings, but the car needed greater visual impact if it were to appeal to a wider audience.

For the tiny microcosm of true performance car enthusiasts, the January 1965 arrival of the Mustang GT350 from Shelby American was as big a deal as the debut of the Ford Mustang to the American automotive universe. Contemporary automobile magazines were enthralled with the GT350 and sang its praises. They described it as "one of the most exciting cars to hit the enthusiast's market in a long time" and "a car that positively exudes character."

Unquestionably, the GT350 offered the enthusiast (the car owner who deliberately sought the most convoluted path from Point A to Point B) an enjoyable experience behind the wheel. But there was also the understanding that the pleasure was not without cost. It was a part of a give-and-take package deal. In exchange for the car's performance, the enthusiast (happily) paid with heavy steering, a stiff clutch, even stiffer brakes, a bone-jarring ride, and side-exiting exhausts that sounded (to

the car's occupants) as though they were routed directly into their ears. The automotive magazines sang the praises of the GT350 and described the machine as "a brute of a car."

Also at issue was the car's appearance. When it was designed, the GT350 was deliberately created with an understated appearance, differing only minimally from the Mustang on which it was based. But despite the car's considerable capabilities (which had to be experienced to be believed), it appeared to be little more than a slightly made-over Mustang. Sales of the first Shelby Mustang suggested that there were more car buyers for whom it was important that the world know that they were driving what looked like a hot car than there were those who didn't care. Even Shelby American recognized the shortcomings of the GT350's Mustang-like appearance, acknowledging that it could have sold more if the car looked less like the Mustang.

1968 Shelby Mustang GT350, GT500 and GT500 KR
In Detail No. 3

SELLING OUT MEANS
SELLING MORE

As Shelby American sat down to plan the second-year GT350, it recognized that the car would have to evolve to survive. "Evolve" actually meant incorporating characteristics that may have been distasteful to Carroll Shelby and the Southern California hot rodders who built the first GT350: refined, soft, and even luxurious. But distasteful or not, it was the first step on an evolutionary journey necessary to ensure the continued survival of the model. They accepted that compromises had to be made in two significant aspects of the GT350: appearance and the rough character that defined the first GT350.

More visual separation from the base Mustang was needed. Shelby accomplished this through the addition of what may well be the two best-known features of any year of the Shelby Mustang: quarter windows and side air scoops. Those design cues, which are iconic today, provided the Shelby with an identity that was

much more visually separated from the Mustang. It was still too easy, however, to characterize the Shelby GT350 as "just a Mustang with stripes" because the two still shared much body sheet metal.

Ford and Shelby made a few more additions to the GT350 that were intended to make the Shelby product more appealing to a larger client base. These included the availability of colors other than white, a rear seat, and an automatic transmission. A conscious effort was made to lower the cost of the car. Some subtractions were made that enthusiasts would likely miss but that the general driving populace would not. These deletions included the Koni shock absorbers, lowered front upper A-arms, and pricey (and noisy) Detroit Locker differential, which were either shifted to the "added cost" column of the window sticker or deleted entirely. The side-exiting low-restriction exhausts also went.

All of these revisions, although perhaps not palatable to true performance enthusiasts, nevertheless had a favorable

Shelby American recognized that, for 1966, its GT350 needed more, not in the performance area, but in the "looks different from a Mustang" area. One of the solutions was a pair of features that have come to be described over the years as "iconic": side scoops and quarter windows. Not only did they differentiate the GT350 from the Mustang, they channeled air to the rear brakes and provided better visibility for the driver. With the GT350 now available with a rear seat (another move to widen the car's appeal), back seaters also enjoyed a better view.

19

Perhaps the most visually significant step of making the Shelby GT350 palatable to a wider consumer base was a softening of the "any color as long as it's white with blue stripes" stance. The first year of "other color" availability saw white/blue as the favorite (red was a close second), although the traditional color scheme experienced a steady decline in popularity for the remainder of the car's existence.

effect on the car's economics. With the same powerplant and underpinnings as the first-year GT350, the 1966 edition still had the flavor of its brash forefather. However, the car was clearly pursuing a path to a softer (and therefore larger) group of enthusiasts. Although it was certainly not to the true performance enthusiasts' taste (and perhaps not even to the manufacturer's), it clearly was appealing to the masses (and to Ford's bottom line); softer was better.

STYLE OVER SUBSTANCE, BY DESIGN

Every year of the Shelby Mustang is unique and can be thought of as a separate step in the car's evolution. Because

they were built some 2,200 miles from the marque's birthplace (and, in fact, by an entirely new and different constructor), the 1968 models are often thought as being *the* turning point in the Shelby Mustang evolution.

There is, of course, some degree of merit to that assessment, but actually, a more solid argument can be made that in 1967, the Shelby Mustang made its largest single evolutionary leap. The car emerged from the design process with a totally unique look that was the greatest stylistic departure from the Ford Mustang (and the Shelby Mustang of the year prior). Moreover, that design process took a completely different approach, one that would have been unthinkable just two years prior.

In late 1966, as the 1967 model was being designed, Shelby American implemented a cost-shifting process. Aftermarket performance features formerly installed by Shelby technicians were replaced by standard Ford components that performed essentially the same job, but which could be installed by Ford on the Mustang assembly line. Ford parts cost less to Shelby American, as did installation by Ford on the Mustang assembly line so the cost-reduction dollars could be used where they would be better seen by the consumer. Shelby deliberately cut corners in the performance department and used the cost savings to buy styling. Shelby-unique performance features were eliminated and instead, lower-cost Ford go-fast features were put on the cars as they rolled down the Mustang assembly line.

Although the 1967 cars had considerably fewer raw performance goodies, the buyer received much more in the all-important styling department. Through the use of multiple fiberglass components, the car sported a nose and tail treatment that was at last unique to the Shelby Mustang. The nose was stretched several inches to give the car a sleek "going a 100 mph"

look even while sitting still, and two center-mounted headlights (the high beams) gave the car a unique face. Wide Cougar taillights graced a rear panel that lay directly beneath a tall, spoilered deck lid.

Inside, for the first time, the Shelby cockpit was based on the deluxe Mustang interior, with thickly padded seats featuring stainless steel trim and hard plastic backs, and with brushed aluminum dash and door panels. Luxury had finally reached the GT350 cockpit; the stark interior of Shelbys of the past was no more. Power steering and power brakes, two features alien to former Shelby buyers, became standard features of the new car and, for the first time, air conditioning (also unthinkable in 1965) was available. This completed the swing from a pure performance car to a luxury performance car and put renewed emphasis on the "grand" in Grand Touring.

However, Shelby American's heightened emphasis on the car's styling should not be taken as a complete abandonment of performance, even though it was no longer performance at the complete exclusion of styling. The 1967 Shelby had, under its sleek, scooped hood, one of the biggest performance enhancements

For 1967, the Shelby GT got what it needed: complete stylistic divorce from its Mustang roots. A whole new nose and tail (unfortunately rendered in ill-fitting fiberglass from multiple, small-run suppliers) made the car look, as Carroll Shelby wanted, "like it was going 100 mph standing still." The '67 Shelby GT was now looked upon as much more than just a Mustang with stripes. The installation of the 428 gave rise to the GT500 and pushed the Shelby GT into the true "muscle car" category.

Owner-added wide blue Le Mans stripes atop a white '68 Shelby harkens back to the days of the first GT350, but the similarity doesn't go beyond the paint job.

ever implemented in the cars from Carroll Shelby: the Ford big-block V-8. The 1967 Shelby GT500 resulted from the infusion of the 428 Police Interceptor engine. The name was completely arbitrary because the car neither possessed nor produced 500 anything; it was actually a result of the horsepower wars during the 1960s in the United States.

Although Ford's Mustang had started the pony car battle, it quickly fell behind because of its Falcon-inspired engine compartment, which was incapable of housing anything larger than a small V-8. The other guys all had 396s, 454s, and 455s. So, for 1967, Ford pumped up the volume in the Mustang's engine room (spatially, not acoustically) to accommodate a 390; Shelby upped the ante to 428. Shelby's Mustang had evolved into a true muscle car.

The 1967 Shelby took a major step toward distinguishing the Shelby GT cars as their own unique entities. The cars no longer looked like minimally made-over Mustangs. In many respects, performance took a back seat to styling, but it wasn't completely left in the dust.

Widening the car's appeal to a broader client base proved to be the ticket for proliferation of the species. However, it was less the successes of the 1967 cars stylistically and more the challenges of turning those styling cues into real hardware that conspired to push Carroll Shelby (not altogether willingly) toward an entirely new way of doing business, and the Shelby Mustang's greatest sales success so far: the 1968 Shelby Cobra GT350, GT500, and GT500 KR.

By 1968, the Shelby Mustang was no longer a bold, brash, rough, and rowdy performance car. It had evolved into an elegant, sophisticated automobile that was more at home rolling up to the grand entrance of a country estate or an exclusive country club than the infield paddock of a racetrack.

PLANNING THE MOST PROLIFIC SHELBY YET

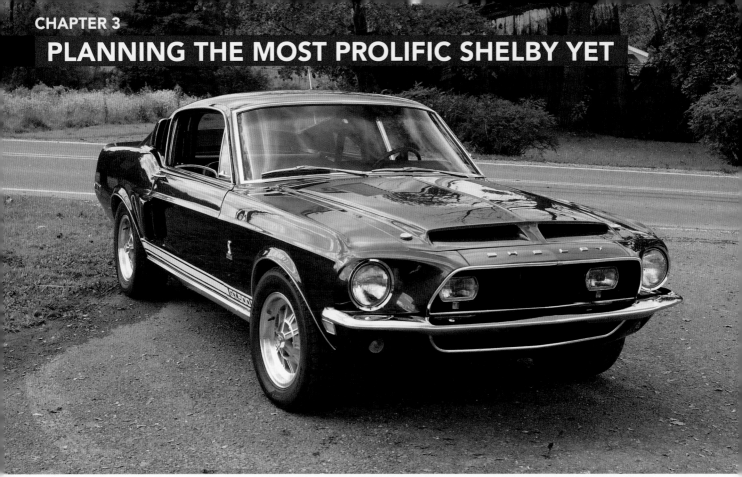

The design and planning cycle for the 1968 Shelby mirrored the approach of the year before. Ford stylists handled the design, only this time at their home studios in Dearborn instead of at Shelby American's Los Angeles facility. Ford Design Center involvement was officially requested on January 16, 1967, when Shelby's general manager, John Kerr, sent a memo to Gene Bordinat, head of the center. That "shopping list" of thoughts and concepts captured what was almost certainly the result of prior discussions and meetings held in Los Angeles. The subject was "STYLING — 1968 SHELBY COBRAS — GT 350 & GT 500" and stated:

"The purpose of this product letter is to request Ford Design Center to proceed at once with the subject program, and, in addition, to provide cost and timing as soon as possible. Following outlines, the scope of the program as presently conceived:

1. EXTERIOR
A. Hood. Revised by dividing present large scoop into two smaller scoops while retaining all normal surfaces in order to require minimum changes to existing molds. In addition, consideration should be given to inclusion of the 1967 GT 500 engine ventilation

Hood louvers were copied from the '67 GT500 hoods in size, shape, and location, although the 1968 set had a slight taper to them. Both GT350s and GT500s (and later, GT500 KRs) had them, although they were intended to be an air-conditioned GT500-only feature in 1967. Once production began, air outlets at the back of the hood were simulated with black decals.

louvers as standard on all vehicles.

B. Grille. New texture and appearance within the existing opening. We suggest investigation of increased usage of bright metal accents either on grille texture or surrounds. While a minimum of change is desired, consideration will be given moving the high-beam lights outboard if this is regarded as appropriate.

C. Lower Back Panel. New to accommodate new tail lights and to incorporate an integral can molded into the fiberglas [sic] panel.

D. Tail Lights. New. It is suggested that this change assume incorporation of a released Ford Motor Company tail light for legal reasons. A narrower, less gross tail light appearance is desired.

E. Brake Scoop. New, if required to conform to 1968 Mustang sheet metal contours.

F. GT Stripes. New. Consideration should be given to a unique GT 500 stripe.

G. Racing Stripes. New.

H. Name Plates, Fender & Desk Appliqués & Gas Cap Insert Panel. New, with emphasis on Cobra emblem and possible use of sea deep plastic.

I. Deck Lid. Consideration should be given to ornamentation or other means of reducing the stark appearance of the flat area below the spoiler and above the lower back panel."

The suggested styling cues emphasized and improved upon the successes of the 1967 model while simultaneously

Tried in 1965 as an experiment for the '66 Shelby, the idea of fitting '65 T-Bird taillights worked better on the '68 Shelby, which had a rear panel especially designed to accept the 'Bird lamps. The silver tail panel and chrome "S-H-E-L-B-Y" lettering added visual interest to the '67 Shelby transom. During the styling evolution, several model-specific designs were tried for fuel cap ornamentation, but in the end, the 1967 style (minus the model designation) was chosen. (Photo Courtesy LegendaryMotorCar.com)

correcting (or at least, deemphasizing) the missteps. Although there is no doubt that Charlie McHose's nose and tail treatment set a new bar for the Shelby's "difference" from the Mustang on which it was based, there was still room for improvement. Opinions differed; some people saw the simple elegance of the rear face; others saw lackluster plainness. The result was a much more stylistically "complicated" transom that maintained the theme of the long, horizontal taillights below a ducktail spoiler.

The new look was achieved with 1965 Thunderbird taillights, which offered more chrome around the red light surface than the previous Cougar lights and the addition of individual letters spelling out "S-H-E-L-B-Y". These, along with a silver-painted taillight panel added more visual interest to the tail end. The legal *faux pas* of the center headlights was also rectified and the

cooling louvers, originally developed for the GT500, became standard equipment on both models. McHose's side scoopery, patterned after the Le Mans–winning MKII racer, was deemed a hit and was transferred to the new model, although without the red brake lights in the upper scoop and air-blowing functionality in the lower.

TOP DOWN, POPULARITY UP

The second half of Kerr's memo continued with a request for a new product, although it was one that had been on Carroll's mind ever since June 1966, when Shelby American's staff meeting minutes reflected that "Four experimental convertibles are being run through the shop at the present time. One of these units is sold and the other three will be used for test purposes in anticipation of a 1967½ GT350 convertible."

The '66 GT350 ragtops quickly became among Shelby's favorite creations and laid the groundwork for the extremely popular '68 Shelby convertibles. The styling request continued:

"As part of the 1968 product plans, Engineering will be requested to release a model 76 convertible. Styling is, therefore, requested to proceed with the following:

A. New Deck Lid. The same as for the fastback, except suitable to the convertible deck opening.
B. New Rear Quarter Extensions. If required to suit model 76 contours. Use of the previously released extensions is most desirable.
C. Unique Built-in Styled Roll Bar. Possible adaptable for down top [sic] use for skis, surfboards, etc.
D. Unique Molded top boot.
E. Unique Landau Cover (Similar to 1962 T-Bird).
F. Unique Vehicle Identification. Possibly as a front fender ornament or a unique GT stripe."

The final sentence of the memo reflected that the clock was ticking: "We request your best as program timing is of the utmost importance."

Additional documentation clarifies and supplements the styling request. For example, it is known that "Ford's best" consisted of at least a trio of stylists: '67 Shelby designer McHose had some input into the new grille opening before handing that end of the car over to boss Gene Bordinat. Stylist John Chun sketched the Shelby-requested hood louvers. However, his designs were ultimately passed over for production because they were felt to mimic, too much, the hood vents on contemporary Chevys. Chun also designed a unique gold "GT500 Cobra" badge to be incorporated into the rocker panel stripe on that model as well as some variations of Ford's contemporary body-side "C" stripe, although neither of those, nor his concepts for "Cobra" and "GT500" gas cap logos, were adopted for production.

History shows what eventually came to fruition and what didn't on the new convertible model. The 1968 convertible did have a styled roll bar but never a landau top or a special molded top boot. Also of particular interest were the small, often-unnoticed chrome eyelets atop the molded rubber covering of the roll bar. They *could* serve a useful purpose in securing skis or a surfboard to the top of the roll bar; that's exactly what they were designed to do. This is graphic evidence that although the '68 Shelby was made in Michigan, it was clearly conceived in California.

TOP LEFT AND RIGHT: The '67 Shelby's lower side air scoop and extractor were carried over to the 1968 model. Sales literature described those features (as well as the ducktail spoiler) as "widely accepted." A. O. Smith's use of more production-line-oriented processes allowed for greater dimensional consistency between components than the hand-laid parts of the year before.

Built as an experiment for the never-released 1967½ Shelby convertible, the last four 1966 GT350s produced were based not on fastbacks, but on HiPo Mustang convertibles. They proved to be very successful. Carroll became especially fond of the ragtops and enjoyed the top-down experience. The quartet of cars laid the groundwork for the very successful 1968 Shelby convertibles. (Photo Courtesy Mark Schwartz)

Although factory literature described one of the functions of the convertible's thickly padded roll bar as a rack for the transportation of skis or a surfboard, virtually none of the Shelby promotional photographs showed a convertible in that mode.

Factory documentation clearly shows that a 1962 Thunderbird-like fiberglass landau top was brought to the design table early on, but it inexplicably disappeared from later plans. A likely and reasonable guess is excessive cost, but it is also possible that someone envisioned that manipulating the top around the padded roll bar during installation or removal wouldn't be easy. The roll bar stayed, but the top went. (Photo Courtesy Scott Nickett)

TOP LEFT:

Shelby American had hoped that the fastback quarter-panel extensions could be used for the new convertible, but the body contours dictated a change in contours for the convertible quarter extensions. The convertible deck lid and quarter extensions, however, were used as-is for the California Special notchbacks.

TOP RIGHT:

The '68 Shelby convertible roll bar was covered in thick, sculptured padding which, when viewed in profile, gave the convertible a targa-like appearance and also served to soften thumps to rear passengers' heads when climbing into the rear seat. The two chrome eyelets atop the convertible's roll bar (manufactured by ACSCO Products of Burbank, California) are often described as being "reportedly" for securing a surfboard to the top of the rubber-covered structure but, as Shelby factory literature described, that's exactly what they were for.

29

Planning the Most Prolific Shelby Yet
Chapter 3

APPEARANCE IS PARAMOUNT

By the end of 1967, Shelby American realized that the Shelby buyer's demographics had shifted considerably. It might be a bit (but not much) of a stretch to say that the current Shelby buyer had evolved into the polar opposite of the first-year customer, but it is certainly true that the 1968 Shelby owner had matured considerably since 1965. The 1968 Shelby buyer was no longer a 20- or 30-something speed freak, but a 50-ish professional, perhaps very likely to have "M.D." or "Esq." following his or her surname.

Evidence of the rapidly changing Shelby owner demographics may be found in the number of cars ordered with automatic transmissions and air conditioning. In 1967, it was 31.7 and 7.9 percent, respectively. Just one model year later, in 1968, those totals had risen to 52.8 and 28.8 percent. The Shelby owner was now more interested in being seen behind the wheel of a stylish automobile than knowing how to turn that wheel to efficiently negotiate, in the words of a 1965 GT350 magazine ad, a "blind-apex closing-radius bend." Performance had clearly taken a back seat to style and Ford and Shelby knew it. Style was now more important than ever and design focused on the smallest details that might negatively impact appearance.

One example of this attention to detail was evident in a late February 1967 memo, in which Shelby American general manager Kerr criticized the appearance of the 1967-type shoulder harness on the upcoming convertible from an appearance standpoint. He directed Engineering to investigate developing a cross-chest harness that emanated from the interior trim panel below the window lower belt line. If that didn't work, a harness that was mounted on the roll bar (as in 1967)

LEFT:
While retracted and with the car's top down, the convertible's cross chest shoulder strap certainly met the requirement to be visually unobtrusive, but even while in use, the strap had a high degree of invisibility.

RIGHT:
The convertible's cross-chest shoulder strap was less effective than a harness suspended from the roll bar, but it was considered aesthetically superior, and that's what mattered. Shelby management was not enamored with the vision of a sleek convertible with shoulder straps dangling from the roll bar (especially parked with the top down on a picturesque sandy beach) so Engineering was directed to devise a cross-chest strap that emanated from the inner quarter panel, below the window line.

The command center of the '68 Shelby was based on the Mustang Interior Décor Group, or deluxe, interior. According to the introductory press release, "The interior will have walnut finish woodgrain appliqués on the instrument panel and door trim. A unique, integral console has been fitted with padded glovebox armrest, auxiliary instruments and driving light switch. The armrest also incorporates an ashtray and courtesy light for the back seat. The steering wheel has a simulated wood rim and a vinyl-covered, padded, safety hub . . ." The deluxe interior's abundant use of wood, even simulated wood, helped convey a sense of luxury and style and also met Shelby American's desire for a "wood" steering wheel, something that had become a Shelby Mustang trademark.

would be acceptable, but with a belt that could be detached at the retractor mount to eliminate the "dangling straps" look of the present harness.

Kerr's memo went on to further direct that if the detachable strap method was preferred (or necessary), it should be fitted to both fastbacks and convertibles. The actual end result was that the convertibles received the cross-chest strap and the fastbacks kept the "danglers," but they were detachable from the retractor mechanism. The suspended harness provided exceptional protection, but there was a desire to implement a less functional alternative because it was more aesthetically pleasing. It was not the same as it was in 1965, when function was

all that mattered. Now, form was clearly calling the shots.

BUT PERFORMANCE STILL MATTERED

If all of this gives the impression that appearance was king, it's not too far from the truth, but that didn't mean that performance had totally abdicated. It still very much existed but it was, however, from a different ruling house. In 1965, when the GT350 debuted, the measure of "performance" was the best time around Riverside Raceway, creature comforts be damned. By 1968, good Shelby performance was defined as a smooth acceleration up to cruising speeds along Rodeo

If a cross-chest shoulder strap for use in the convertible wouldn't fly, the second-best choice was a suspended harness that detached from the retractors so the unsightly straps hanging from the roll bar weren't visible. The decision was that if Plan B was the path followed, it was to be used on both the convertible and fastback models; somewhat unusually, the convertibles received the cross-chest belt and the hardtops received detachable straps. The two-piece straps meant passengers entering and exiting the rear seat of the fastbacks were less likely to become entangled in the straps.

Although automobile enthusiasts saw the interior of the Shelby Cobra as the perfectly efficient place from which to pilot the monster-engined roadster, the feds likely saw a lethal killing zone with little or no crash protection for the occupants. Carroll Shelby realized that there was no way to bring the Cobra into safety compliance for 1968 and he wisely chose to discontinue the two-seater rather than to turn it into a mere shadow of its former self to comply with governmental regulations. The car might have been dead; the Cobra name wasn't.

TOP RIGHT:

Despite a thorough check of federal motor vehicle regulations to assess the new '68 Shelby's compliance, Shelby Automotive was bitten (again) with a lighting issue. Some states mandated that only a single flashing light constituted a turn signal; the sequential blinkers on the rear of the cars violated that rule. Dealers soon received instructions on how to "un-sequentialize" the lights.

Drive. The times, for Carroll Shelby and his cars, had clearly changed.

In February 1967, a memo from Kerr to the company engineering staff stated, in part, "As you know, there has been some dissatisfaction with the performance of the 1967 model GT500. For 1968, it is our intention that the GT500 be not the equal of, but must be superior to the Pontiac GTO and other comparable vehicles."

This memo led to the testing and adoption of the single 4-barrel carburetor atop the GT500's 428, which did yield better and smoother performance than the 1967's twin Holleys. The recommendation to investigate "alternative induction systems using fuel injection or a blower" was followed on the '68 Green Hornet

notchback prototype (along with an independent rear suspension), but neither was adopted for production.

Another aspect of the 1968 cars that was discussed was conformance to state and federal motor vehicle regulations. Just a few weeks earlier, Shelby American was being reamed by motor vehicle inspectors in multiple states for multiple violations of 1967 vehicle lighting laws. To that end, "Engineering is requested to determine if there are any federal safety regulations effective in 1968, which are not satisfied by the Mustang as supplied by San Jose.

"Engineering is further requested to determine state legal regulations and requirements, which must be satisfied to permit acceptance of the GTs as marketable vehicles by state regulatory agencies."

After the fiascos of inboard headlights being too close together and brake lights being too high to be legal, Shelby wanted to be positioned to deliver legally accepted vehicles nationwide after learning firsthand that the adage, "It is better to seek forgiveness than ask permission," didn't work well with motor vehicle folks. Shelby American's check of impending legal conformance, although yielding a "we're in pretty good shape" for the Mustang, had a devastating effect on another of its signature products.

THE "SHELBY COBRA" LIVES ON (SORT OF)

As early as the 1967 model year, it was apparent to Shelby (the man as well as the company) that the upcoming 1968 federal motor vehicle safety standards would sound the death knell for the Cobra. A whole litany of crash protection measures, mandated by the government, created a new safety standard that the Cobra didn't have the slightest hope of passing. Because of the nature of the beast (a description carefully chosen), the Cobra was not even a candidate for upgrading to meet the new standards. It was a bitter pill to swallow, but the handwriting on the wall was abundantly clear: 1967 would be the last year that Carroll Shelby could legally build the car with which he had become synonymous. All good things truly did have to end.

Even though production of the Cobra ended in 1968, Shelby implemented a bit of creative marketing to keep the name in the performance automobile spotlight. The 1968 Shelby being constructed by Shelby Automotive would be known as the "Shelby Cobra GT" and would be available as the Shelby Cobra GT350 and Shelby Cobra GT500 (and later, the Shelby Cobra GT500 KR). Even if Carroll

Shelby could no longer build the Cobra, he still could, in a manner of speaking.

CHANGE OF VENUE

As style and design questions of the '68 Shelby were dealt with, a larger, more all-encompassing problem needed attention: where, how, by whom, and to how many cars was this going to take place? In the simplest of terms, Shelby American became Shelby Automotive, moved to Michigan, and built cars there. But to simply leave it at that without discussing, at least to some level of detail, all the factors leading to that result is much like bypassing several hundred pages of a skillfully crafted murder mystery to jump ahead to the last page just to find out that the butler did it.

In the literal sense, Shelby's new home was a destination, but in a figurative sense, the move was a journey, the details of which are complex and interrelated. Shelby American's move to Michigan can best be described as a very complex answer to a relatively simple question.

A PERFECT STORM

In some ways, the gradual piling up of issues that contributed to Shelby's relocation began the very first time that one of his Cobras took the high spot on the finisher's podium. The problem was that the cars were "Shelby Cobras" and although they were "powered by Ford," they weren't "Ford Cobras." Henry II and his organization dumped lots of cash into Shelby's operation in the quest for road racing dominance. After all that expense, in Ford's eyes, Ford only received second billing, and that bugged Ford. That may seem petty and trivial, but to Ford, it was anything but.

Another source of some animosity may also have stemmed from the fact that Shelby and Ford operated very differently. Ford had established processes and procedures for everything, whereas when something needed to be done, Shelby just went out and did it. Although he certainly got the job done, the Ford "suits" always thought of him and his distant operation as a loose cannon. These corporate personality differences contributed to a feeling that Shelby and his run-amok organization needed tighter control. Those philosophical differences in modus operandi were the impetus toward a concerted effort to move Carroll Shelby and his operation closer to the source of his funding.

Shelby's very different way of doing business may have contributed to a vague and nebulous feeling that Ford didn't have adequate control of its junior partner, but very tangible events occurred in the fall of 1966 that started the relocation snowball rolling in earnest. In October, Fred Goodell was hired as Shelby American's chief engineer to oversee engineering operations in Los Angeles. Both Fred and John Kerr were Ford guys and one of their objectives (whether Carroll knew it or not) was to bring Shelby under tighter Blue Oval control.

Fred's arrival at Shelby American coincided with the start of '67 Shelby production, which soon became quite problematic. The main issue was Shelby American's small fiberglass parts sup-

plier base. There were several suppliers but none with the capacity to fulfill the entire 1967 parts order, so production had to be split over several small vendors. When the parts arrived, there was a great deal of inconsistency between parts from different suppliers, and dimensional dissimilarity between parts from the same manufacturer.

Adding insult to injury was the fact that the steel body that Ford supplied to Shelby American for making the molds for the fiberglass parts was distorted from previous testing. All of those inconsistent-quality parts were made from twisted molds pulled from a twisted master. When the parts were fitted on cars with straight bodies, the result was predictable: considerable hand-fitting of the parts was necessary to achieve an acceptable fit.

Fred often gets credit for implementing production-line techniques at Shelby during the 1967 build, but Shelby American's extremely capable production manager, Jack Khoury, did an exceptional job under very difficult circumstances. The story is often told that '67 Shelby production was a complete fiasco. Actually, 1967 production wasn't nearly the disaster it was made out to be. In the same 11-month production period as '66 GT350 production, Shelby American built almost 1,000 more 1967 cars. Ford, however, wanted many more than the 3,300 1968 cars produced. Despite being extremely capable fabricators, Shelby American wasn't a mass production shop with the capacity to satisfy Ford's production plans. A more efficient source with greater production output was needed.

A couple of other ingredients added to the "move Shelby to Michigan" snowball. The San Jose plant expressed some reluctance to continue supplying Mustang platforms to Shelby American for conversion to GT350s and GT500s, citing disruptions to its normal production output. A new Mustang supplier was sought. The Metuchen, New Jersey, assembly plant, had enough production capacity so as not to "miss" figurative handfuls of cars (compared to their total output) going to Shelby. And although it was recognized that Metuchen was a long haul from Los Angeles, it was much closer to a new Shelby location in, say, Michigan.

Another factor that gave Shelby American a definite shove toward Michigan was the impending end to the company's lease on hangars from North American Aviation at Los Angeles International Airport. The two cavernous hangars had been home to Carroll Shelby and the Cobras, GT40s, and Mustangs since approximately January 1965 but in September 1967, North American got its buildings back, leaving Shelby American theoretically homeless. Had any number of the other factors not come into play, Ford (or Shelby) could have easily located new digs in Southern California but, just as one Lilliputian was a non-issue to Gulliver but many were a different matter entirely, the deck became increasingly stacked against Shelby staying in the Golden State. Shelby was the victim of a convergence of factors that pushed him and his company to move and resistance became increasingly futile. Ironically, however happenstance, and not Ford's corporate manipulation, sealed the deal for Shelby's move out of California.

A. O. SMITH

Shelby's general manager, John Kerr, hit upon a potential source for 1968 production, more or less by the result of a set of random circumstances. John was a friend of George Macfarlane, who was the sales and engineering manager of Smith Plastics, located conveniently in Ionia, Michigan, driving distance from Dearborn. This company was a subsidiary of the larger A. O. Smith Corporation. Smith Plastics had, for more than a decade, fabricated various fiberglass components for the automobile industry, ranging from small parts to entire Chevrolet Corvette bodies.

Smith had just had a stroke of bad luck when Chevy decided to bring Corvette body production under its own roof,

In addition to the Shelby Cobra program, A. O. Smith also installed sunroofs on Cougars, which was included as part of their contract with Shelby Automotive and Ford. Two examples of its handiwork were displayed at the Ionia plant's main entrance for a while in 1968. (Photo Courtesy Jack Redeker)

Sheet molding compound (SMC), made up of ground fiberglass, resin, and fillers, and is analogous, both in consistency and concept to cookie dough, is laid into one of the mold halves. The mold halves are closed and heat and pressure are applied. After curing, the mold is opened, the part removed, and the edges trimmed. The process yields a finished component of exceptional dimensional stability and part-to-part consistency. An added bonus is that the underside of components such as the hood and deck lid present a more finished and "professional" appearance because they are formed in their own half of the mold.

Discussions between Shelby American and A. O. Smith began in early 1967 when Fred Goodell sat down with George Macfarlane for a series of investigatory meetings. Goodell wanted to determine Smith's capabilities without Macfarlane finding out that Goodell was interested in them. The two went to extremes to ensure that neither hand was tipped. Fred's visits to Smith bordered on the cloak-and-dagger.

By May, A. O. Smith had prepared and submitted a proposal for the production of the 1968 Shelby GT350 and GT500 (in fastback, convertible, *and* hardtop body styles) for the next successive model years through 1971. As is often the case with proposal submissions, the offeror (in this case, Smith) submitted pricing for several production quantities, based on some guidance as to what the tentative production quantities would be. Those quantities indicated that Shelby and Ford (especially) had high hopes for

A. O. Smith used matched metal molds, which gave a much better lineup between the multiple panels, especially up front, on any given car and better car-to-car consistency of panel fit than in 1967. Unlike the '67 Shelby, where the fiberglass parts were literally hand-fitted to each car, 1968 fiberglass was truly interchangeable among cars.

leaving Smith with no source of future income. Kerr's friendship with Macfarlane, Smith's location, coupled with its newfound excess production capacity, and also perhaps a willingness to talk a business deal, all conspired to create a tractive force that pulled Shelby toward Michigan.

One of the real benefits of Smith was that to almost the same degree that Shelby American wasn't a mass production house, Smith was. It had the facilities, the workforce, and the experience to deliver just what Ford wanted: Shelby Mustangs, in quantity and with quality.

Smith used a considerably more sophisticated molding technique than Shelby's multiple California fiberglass vendors, known as "matched metal molding." As the name implies, the process made use of two metal molds, one for the outer surface of the part, and one for the inner. The molds are machined so that when closed, the space between them determined the thickness of the fabricated part.

1968 Shelby Mustang GT350, GT500 and GT500 KR
In Detail No. 3

future Shelby Mustang production. The quantity bids were 6,000, 8,000, 10,000, and 12,000 cars annually.

Several revisions of the proposal went back and forth and by early in the second half of 1967, terms were finalized for the production of the 1968 Shelby. A. O. Smith would be basically responsible for three phases of Shelby production: it would fabricate the components; it would paint and install them on the vehicles; and it would finish the vehicles by adding ornamentation and decoration, such as badges, fuel caps, and grille trim.

Shelby's responsibility included running gear (engines, suspensions, brakes), styling and design of Shelby-unique components (roll bar, fog light installation, interior appointments), and the design of the badging, emblems, and markings that Smith would install to finish the cars.

Ford had overall program responsibility and determined how many vehicles of each body style would be built.

In the midst of the back-and-forth negotiations and discussions between Shelby American, Ford, and A. O. Smith, another event occurred in the spring of 1967. Automaker/race car builder/parts and accessories manufacturer Shelby American split into three separate entities. The trisection resulted in the Shelby Racing Company and the Shelby Parts Company remaining in California, but Shelby Automotive moved east and was headquartered in Southfield, Michigan.

Shelby Automotive also maintained engineering offices and a shop in Ionia, to oversee A. O. Smith production. It was housed in a former Buick dealership and

garage. Shelby American still existed on the organizational chart but effectively was a "holding company" for the other branches. For the first time since he started building automobiles in 1962, Carroll Shelby (or his company) no longer built the automobiles that carried his name.

THE VISION BECOMES REALITY

Whether it is argued that the construction of full-up promotional prototype vehicles represents the final phase of the design process, or the first of the production, semantics aside, the build of these creations launch the process of introducing the formerly secret design concepts

The Lime Gold 67-00439 was transformed, courtesy of a hand-built set of 1968 Shelby fiberglass components, into the Acapulco Blue promotional prototype '68 GT500 fastback. Clues to the car's prototype status are the single-piece nose (sans the production seams flanking the "S-H-E-L-B-Y" lettering) and the twist-lock hood fasteners with retention lanyards. (Photo Courtesy LegendaryMotorCar.com)

In its initial incarnation, the '68 Shelby prototype convertible wore Candy Apple Red paint and rolled on aluminum 10-spoke wheels. An early rocker panel stripe incorporated a gold "GT500" badge within the stripe. The ragtop soon gained a Wimbledon White paint job for photographic purposes as well as fake mag wheel covers. Another interim stripe/emblem scheme had an unbroken side stripe and individual chrome "G-T-5-0-0" letters at mid-fender height; these gave way to the coiled snake and "Cobra" badge. (Photo Courtesy Jerry Heasley)

Considered popular features, the side scoops and rear deck spoiler from the '67 Shelby carried over to the 1968 cars. The rear-quarter marker light was new for 1968 (to conform to motor vehicle safety standards) and was initially dummied-up on the prototype cars as actual units weren't available from Ford when the cars were built. The new-for-1968 wheel lip moldings were fitted, but the bright aluminum rocker moldings weren't, another tipoff to the car's prototype status. (Photo Courtesy LegendaryMotorCar.com)

to the general public. These hand-built creations come to life long before the first production example ("Job One") even begins its journey down the production line. One of the reasons for the early birth was to accommodate the long lead times of the layout and printing cycle of the then-current automobile print media.

If there was a downside to the expansion of the Shelby product line to include a convertible, it was that now two types of long-lead promotional vehicles were needed. To showcase the fastback body style of the 1968 line, a '67 GT500, which did duty as a Shelby American engineering vehicle (No. 00463, the Lime Gold GT500 on which the louvered hood was first tested) was selected; the 1968 convertible was based on a Candy Apple Red big-block '67 Mustang convertible.

Planning and development was already underway and Ford Styling had just completed the clay workups of the new components when construction of the two 1968 promotional cars began around April 1967. This was approxi-

mately six months before the planned production of Job One. It represented the end of an era, as the build of the 1968 prototypes was the last new vehicle development performed at Shelby American's Los Angeles facility. A nearly $15,000 set of hand-built prototype components that included two hoods and noses, two deck lids and matching end caps, and two consoles had been received from A. O. Smith a month before. A prototype padded roll bar was also fabricated for the convertible.

No. 00463 received a coat of Acapulco Blue paint. Initially, the convertible stayed in its "as-delivered" red (although it was soon painted Wimbledon White for a better appearance in the predominantly black-and-white automobile magazines of the day). The two cars were taken to various scenic locations around Southern California for photo shoots, visiting the San Jacinto mountain range, Malibu Beach, and the Hollywood Park horse track. That the '68 Shelby was an essential tool of the jet-setter was suggested by a photo shoot at a local airport alongside one of the most recognizable status symbols of the day, a brand-new Lear Jet.

In early July, the two cars were officially introduced to the automotive press at the Long-Lead Technical Conference held at Riverside Raceway. Although the invitation-only attendees were admonished not to release any photos or details of the cars until their October debut, the very next month, magazines started hinting that rumors of a long-hoped-for Shelby convertible for 1968 might just be true.

Just as prototypes evolve into production models, the Shelby promotional vehicles also underwent a sort of evolution within their prototype status. In the time between the cars' debut in April and their appearances at Riverside in July, subtle changes occurred periodically in the badging and ornamentation. These

small details identified the prototype cars at various times in their evolution, but the overall design of the car's styling changed very little from prototype to production. The 1968 Shelby Cobra GT was ready for production. But was production ready for the 1968 Shelby Cobra GT?

PRODUCTION BEGINS . . . SLOWLY

Over the years, production of the '67 Shelbys at Los Angeles has come to be described with words such as "debacle" or "disastrous" while, conversely, the 1968 build is often thought of as the epitome of automobile production running on autopilot, completely devoid of issues and hiccups. In general terms, 1968 production was orders of magnitude smoother than the production program of the year before. In actuality, the build of the Shelby Cobra GTs by A. O. Smith was not the voyage across the waveless sea; more than one wave crashed over the bow both before and during actual production.

The Mustang-to-Shelby conversion process has just begun as a Wimbledon White Cobra Jet fastback begins its journey down A. O. Smith's assembly-line trolley. Unlike "straight-line" assembly at Shelby American's Los Angeles facility where the car dollies had to be returned to the start of the line as each car was completed, Smith's circulated continuously. (Photo Courtesy Jack Redeker)

Near the end of the conversion process for a red GT500 KR convertible, a newly completed Shelby Cobra lacks wheels, Cobra Jet air-cleaner assembly, and a few small finishing details (such as the chrome nose letters) before proceeding to final inspection and, if necessary, repair for any defects from the assembly process. Additional cost issues arose, but A. O. Smith's basic cost for Shelby Cobra conversion was right around $580 per car, very close to the 1967 proposal. (Photo Courtesy Jack Redeker)

The first 1968 Mustang rolled out the door of the Metuchen, New Jersey, assembly plant on August 16, 1967. However, just as the huge factory was about to settle into the routine of disgorging Mustangs of all colors and configurations (some of which were bound for A. O. Smith in Michigan), disaster struck. The United Auto Workers' (UAW) contract with Ford was up for renewal and after it became apparent that the Blue Oval and the union weren't exactly on the same page, the UAW struck Ford beginning on September 6, just as 1968 Mustang production started to hit its stride.

The strike dragged on until Veteran's Day. Shelby production in November was pretty much nil and even December's was nothing to write home about. The strike delayed Shelby's Job One by more than six weeks, although in the grand scheme of things, it didn't matter much. Even if Metuchen had delivered cars to Shelby per the original schedule, A. O. Smith was way behind the power curve ramping up to full-scale production. Dealers didn't start receiving '68 Shelbys until nearly two full months after the car's early October public introduction. It was an inauspicious

beginning to the latest chapter in the continuing story of Carroll Shelby and his automobiles.

If production startup had its issues, so did production once it settled into a routine. In January, for example, a memo titled "Production Difficulties at A. O. Smith, Ionia" was written for Shelby Automotive General Manager John Kerr, describing various production failings at the plant. One of the nagging issues reflected the manufacturing culture in 1960s America.

In those days, production quantity was ever-important; production quality was far less so ("Quality is Job 1" banners didn't hang from the rafters of Ford manufacturing plants for more than a decade later). One example (and a continuing source of trouble) concerned the fit of the upper air extractors on the fastbacks that were assembled, painted, and installed on the cars without verification that the scoops were of acceptable quality. Issues were found at final inspection, by which time all the interior trim had been assembled on the cars; those with bad extractors required a complete disassembly of all inside componentry. Shelby repeatedly recommended that the extractors be checked *before* installation but Smith continued "business as usual" until the end of production.

Another recurring issue was that despite the installation of two state-of-the-art (and costly) engine analyzers at the end of the production line (which were intended to set engine specifications per government emissions standards), the expensive machines sat idle most of the time.

Removal of sheet metal between the Mustang's triple taillight openings in the cars' rear fascia was also problematic. The operation was repeatedly performed with hand tools (despite nearby power shears and snips that would both speed up and neaten the operation).

A new element to the 1968 Shelby production was never before encountered by Shelby or Ford: a third party. That third party was A. O. Smith and it was under contract to perform a very specific set of tasks; it would be paid only for performance of those tasks. From the start, Smith had to perform unplanned (read "unpriced") deviations from its proposal.

At the onset of production, although production tooling was used, hand-layup of more than 300 hoods was required to get the production ball rolling. This required more skilled labor grades than were required for automated production, thus, higher labor costs were incurred in the build of those hoods.

Production start-up wasn't the only area where extra costs were incurred. Smith also had to perform extra work to bring the Metuchen-supplied Mustangs to the point where they were supposed to be when they arrived in Ionia, that is, complete, functional cars. The Mustangs fell a bit short of this mark (although quality, functionality, and completeness problems also existed on Dearborn-supplied Cougars, on which Smith installed sunroofs, also under the Shelby contract).

Mustang defects included a large group of GT500 KRs; more than 160 cars required removal and relocation of the heat riser tube on the air-cleaner assem-bly. Some GT350 carburetors also had to be replaced because the incorrect units were installed on the Metuchen line. The list of defects needing correction was as varied as it was long: inoperative lights and other electrical components (inside and out, of all types); missing parts included oil dipsticks, fan shrouds, under-carpet sound deadener, power steering dipsticks, inside door handles, fog light switches, hood rubber seals, sun visor knobs, tailpipe hangers, and (somewhat incredibly), the occasional windshield wiper arm. Speedometers, oil senders, and, occasionally, front shock absorbers of the wrong type, as well as alternators, tilt steering wheels, heater blowers, power steering pumps, and Thermactor pumps didn't work, leaked, or were noisy and had to be replaced.

These all incurred costs not included by Smith in its initial proposal to Shelby.

"DING IN ROOF"

Production of the '68 Shelbys introduced several new constituents to the broth that were never present before. One

Some sort of protection against the elements for the Mustangs' engine compartments and trunks were needed for the two-day railcar trip from Metuchen to Ionia. Damaged and/or otherwise unusable Mustang and Shelby hoods and deck lids were pressed into service as temporary covers to keep out rain and snow. This quickly composed snapshot highlights a typical view of the cars in their temporary storage areas. (Photo Courtesy Jack Redeker)

Unforeseen, however, was the damage that Mustangs on the upper decks of railcars received at the hands of pebble-throwing children as the trains rumbled across the states from New Jersey into Michigan. "Ding in roof" was frequently noted on incoming cars' inspection reports and created headaches for A. O. Smith, which had to repair the dents. Although somewhat difficult to see with the lighting in this snapshot, there appears to be one of three WT 5185 orange fastbacks on the middle deck of this railcar. (Photo Courtesy Jack Redeker)

of them, completely foreseen or planned for, was the much greater distance from the Ford plant building Shelby's Mustang platforms to the Shelby site performing the work. In Southern California, it was a one-day trip from Ford's San Jose assembly plant to Shelby American in Los Angeles. This meant that the cars could be transported essentially as they left San Jose, with missing hoods and deck lids and quarter louvers. The almost-always-sunny weather meant that no additional precautions had to be taken against foul weather entering the open interiors and engines because there really wasn't any foul weather.

But the two-day train trip from the Metuchen assembly plant in New Jersey to A. O. Smith in Michigan (especially in winter) was another matter entirely. The cars couldn't sit overnight on rail sidings with open engine compartments and trunks. To keep the weather out, temporary measures were taken: defective Mustang and/or Shelby hoods (and deck lids) were installed temporarily at Metuchen for the train trip to Ionia. There was, however, an unexpected element to

the greater travel distance from Metuchen to Ionia that caused multiple production headaches and had consequences that remained long after the last Shelby Cobra rolled out of A. O. Smith: children.

Multiple occurrences of "ding in roof" (and correspondingly, "hole in roof" on convertibles) were noted by A. O. Smith as the cars were offloaded at Ionia, resulting from the cars being pelted by pebbles thrown by children as entertainment as the trains rumbled across Pennsylvania, Ohio, Indiana, and Michigan. The end result, irrespective of cause, was that all of those dings and holes required repair (and therefore, additional cost) on the part of Smith.

Rather than interrupt production while each cost overrun was negotiated, Smith kept the line chugging along with plans to submit the overcharges to Ford/Shelby to be paid at a later date. Unbeknown to Smith, however, Ford and Shelby opportunistically saw this as "unauthorized" deviation from their contract and when the time came to discuss the payment of those costs, Smith was criticized for incurring the unplanned costs.

Discussions of the extra costs continued well into 1969, but because the costs had already been incurred and the contract under which they were incurred long since terminated, Smith was forced to accept negotiated levels of payment that didn't exactly add up to its actual expenditures. In effect, Ford and Shelby had Smith over a barrel and Smith had to take what was offered, or leave it, even if it wasn't entirely palatable (or, frankly, fair).

Shelby's Kerr and Smith's Macfarlane, by virtue of their respective job descriptions, had to look out for their own company's best interests, and this necessitated a somewhat adversarial professional relationship. But their personal friendship kept a certain level of civility in the otherwise-contentious cost discussions. It wouldn't be difficult to imagine, however, that their friendship was likely put to the test during these negotiations.

IT'S THE ECONOMY, STUPID

The adage "it's the bullet you don't see that gets you" could almost have been coined especially for 1968 Shelby Cobra GT production. A thorough investigation of A. O. Smith as a production house and thoughtful incorporation of styling positives into the car's design were meant to guarantee success beyond that achieved previously. However, something unforeseen reared its head and actually forced a premature termination of '68 Shelby production: the economy. History books reflect that the year-long recession of 1969–1970 began in the fall of 1969 but the earliest signs of economic downturn actually began to manifest themselves in late 1966.

By 1968, still pre-recession by definition, economic slowdown had reached the point of being considered "significant" by economists and that slowdown (with its associated inflation, unemployment, and a general lack of consumer confidence) began to affect sales of things not considered essential by consumers. This belt-tightening extended to all manner of discretionary purchases and certainly didn't exclude costly luxury performance

automobiles. Even as '68 Shelbys first started hitting the showroom floor, concerns were voiced by dealers who attempted to push those not-inexpensive vehicles on a now-cautious public that just wasn't buying pricey sports cars.

The varying quantities in A. O. Smith's proposal allowed for production (supply) to be tailored to what turned out to be an optimistically high consumer demand forecast for the cars that never materialized. Stalled sales didn't justify even the lowest planned-for production quantity and when the 4,450th Shelby rolled off the Ionia production line, it was the last. It can't be said for sure just when the decision to halt production was made. What is certain is that the eventual production quantity was nowhere in the plan and, in fact, fell far short of even the most pessimistic anticipation of production totals.

Although Shelby, Ford, and A. O. Smith each brought considerable competence and capability to the table in their respective areas of expertise, unfortunately, economic clairvoyance wasn't one of them.

As slow as sales of '68 Shelbys were, sales of the '69s were even slower. Ford's introduction of other performance vehicles such as the Cobra Jet, BOSS, and Mach I (which offered equal or better performance at lower cost) plus a U.S. economy that had tanked, doomed sales of the relatively pricey Shelbys to sub-lackluster levels. By the end of the 1969 model year, Carroll Shelby had his fill of corporate politics and asked to be released from his Mustang contract two years early; Ford agreed. (Photo Courtesy Jack Redeker)

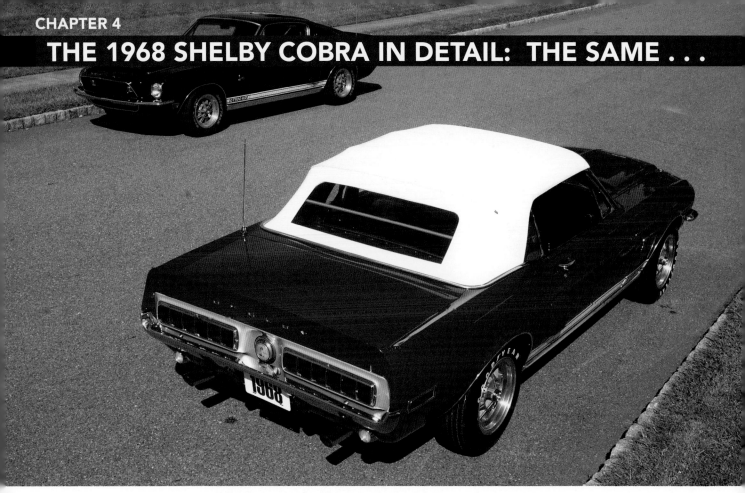

The fact that the '68 Shelby was built in Michigan gives the impression that it was a totally new car and a complete departure from the marque's Southern California roots. In fact, it has more tie-in to the beach at Malibu than most enthusiasts realize. The car was actually conceived in the Golden State and the first promotional prototypes were constructed at Shelby American's Los Angeles facility; they were the last Shelby Mustangs built there. Sidestepping the perception created by the newness of the Michigan build and taking a good, unbiased look at the car reveals that while there are new aspects to the car, there are also traces of the familiar contained therein, both on and under the skin. The new Shelby was something old and also something new.

KEEPING IT SIMPLE(R)

On a '67 Shelby, there were four places where identification unique to the model had to be installed as well as three uniquely sized wheel center decals, one for each of the available three types of wheel. For 1968, general badging was simplified. A unique "GT350" or "GT500" emblem appeared in only once place, on

BUT DIFFERENT

the dash, above the glove compartment. (As in 1967, model designation was also made via the side stripe decal). A more generic "Shelby Cobra" gas cap logo was devised, patterned after the 1967 type but sans the model designation, eliminating the need for a unique decal for each model.

Only one type of wheel was offered by the factory, as opposed to a trio the year before. Now, it was only a simulated mag-type wheel cover, which is often mis-identified by the much snappier moniker of "hubcap". Unlike the rebadged Thunderbird wheel cover of 1967, the 1968 wheel cover was generic, neither a Ford nor Shelby product. Manufactured by Garwood Industries of Ypsilanti, it was also available as optional equipment on Chevrolet Impalas, Chevelles, and Novas. The wheel cover was a heavy die-cast or stamped piece that had a strong resemblance to the 1965 Shelby Cragar wheel. It featured

OPPOSITE:

Perhaps the biggest news for 1968 was the availability of both the GT350 and GT500 in the Model 76 (convertible) body style, complementing the existing Model 63 fastback. Just as when tried experimentally a couple of years earlier, the ragtop Shelby proved to be very popular with nearly 3 out of every 10 cars built having soft tops. Consumers were offered a choice of either black or white (called "Parchment") tops on the '68s and all were power-actuated with glass folding rear windows.

The promotional prototype '68 Shelbys debuted with lanyarded "R" pins securing the hood. By the time production kicked off, the pins were replaced with twist locks developed by Tom McIntyre of ACSCO Products as an engineering school project. The locks protruded above the surface of the hood when unlocked, providing a visual indication of their lock/unlock status.

The '68 Shelby Cobra retained the stock Mustang hood-latching mechanism in addition to the two twist locks. The striker mount also served as an attachment place for supports for the fiberglass nose, which had now become a three-segment affair; the gaps between the segments were styled as deliberate seams. As in 1967, a power steering fluid cooler (a '65 Galaxie component) was mounted to the front of the radiator support, albeit vertically this year.

RIGHT: Although early plans were for a unique "GT500" side stripe, in the end both that model and the GT350 used the same stripes as the '67 Shelbys, although the 1968 designations were once again centered on the fender bottoms (not pushed back against the door edge as on the 1967 cars). Another distinguishing feature of the production '68 Shelbys (both fastback and convertible) was the use of bright aluminum wheel lip moldings and rocker moldings.

a center cap made just for Shelby that accepted the fuel cap decal as its center cap logo (even more simplification). The wheel cover was the only wheel available for the 1968 Shelby from the factory although optional cast aluminum 10-spoke wheels were added by dealers or later by individual owners. (These are the same design as in 1967 but rede-

signed on the backside to clear the '68 Mustang's floating brake caliper.)

Production records show that almost all of the 1968 Shelby builds left A. O. Smith with wheel covers. The only "factory" exceptions were a half dozen or so cars bound for export sales, where presumably rougher roads led to the cars shedding their Garwood hubcaps.

LEFT: A more three-dimensional snake fender badge was designed by ACSCO Products, in conjunction with Ford. Mr. Shelby favored the more "Tiffany" (as he called it) appearance of the new emblem over the flat 1967 type. There was not a passenger- and driver-side ornament; as a result, the snake faced rearward on one side of the car and forward on the other.

LEFT: As with the wheel covers, the radio antenna was packaged in the car's trunk upon shipment out of A. O. Smith and installed by the dealer as part of their pre-delivery inspection. On some early cars, dealers erroneously installed the mast in the stock Mustang location on the passenger-side front fender instead of the prescribed Shelby location on the driver-side rear quarter panel. Some of these "misplaced" antennas were relocated to the prescribed place under warranty (the upfront location made radio reception poor because of the fiberglass hood), but some cars never received the relocation and still have antennas in their original "wrong" location today.

TOP: As in 1967, the '68 Shelby used the complete, stock Mustang GT exhaust system. Also, as with the year before, chrome tips were added to the tailpipes. The 1968 version was the same size and shape as the 1967 item but had a unique "pipe within a pipe" design.

MIDDLE: With the solid-lifter High Performance 289 having been discontinued the year before, the '68 GT350 was pushed along by a hydraulic-lifter 302. The engines were basically stock 302s with steel oil pans and cast-iron exhaust manifolds. Some early GT350 302s retained their "as-built by Ford" cast-iron intakes and Autolite carburetors because the Cobra/Holley combination hadn't been emissions certified when GT350 production began. As in 1967, the one-piece "export brace" returned, running from the shock towers to the firewall. (Photo Courtesy Colin Comer)

BOTTOM: The Police Interceptor 428 made a curtain call as the powerplant for the '68 Shelby GT500 but rated at five more ponies than the year before; more efficient carburetion (a single 715-cfm Holley atop an aluminum Ford intake) helped. Both the GT350 and GT500 used the late-1967 style of oval aluminum air cleaner (although sitting atop a single carburetor on both models). Access to the distributor on all models except GT350 with automatic transmission was hindered by the Thermactor air bypass valve plumbing.

For the fourth year running, the GT350 engine was topped off by an aluminum Cobra intake (the 1967 version with S7MS parts identification), but a Holley 600-cfm carburetor resided atop the intake in place of the previous year's 715. GT350s used the mid-1966 and later die-cast "Cobra Powered by Ford" valvecovers; the GT500's rockers were capped by black Cobra Le Mans valvecovers.

All '68 Shelbys used modified shock absorber "beehives" with washers welded to the tops to increase the bearing surface of the shock absorber attaching bolts.

Electrical feed to the console-mounted ammeter was provided through the use of a junction block, sourced from the Mercury parts bin. This is the same part as was used on later 1967 Shelbys.

As in 1967, the '68 Shelby interior was based on the Mustang Interior Décor Group (aka, "deluxe") cockpit. Also as in 1967, a second, lighter interior color choice (in addition to black) was offered. Called "Saddle," the beige color was complemented with darker brown carpet and dash pad and was used in just under 15 percent of the '68 Shelby builds. The Tilt-Pop steering column (a "mandatory option" on most cars) was adjustable in "tilt" through nine driving positions. When the ignition was shut off and the driver's door opened, the wheel "popped" up and to the right to allow easier ingress into/egress from the driver's seat. An interlock prevented the engine from starting with the wheel "popped."

The solution to the missing oil pressure gauge and ammeter in the deluxe Mustang instrument cluster was solved by the installation of the gauges under the dash, but this year, they were neatly integrated into a carpeted, full-length floor console. Although it was planned to incorporate the driving light switches into the console, the standard Mustang GT underdash fog-light switch was used; convertibles had the power top control knob adjacent. GT350s and GT500s with automatic transmissions kept their Ford-installed vinyl-covered shift levers (the covering was part of the Interior Décor Group).

Shelbys with a 4-speed transmission adopted a shift knob from the Ford accessory catalog as their standard.

BELOW: Immediately aft of the belt clips, the Shelby-unique console swept upward to form a storage compartment between the front seats, topped off with a padded door/armrest that had an embossed "Shelby Cobra" logo on it.

LEFT: Further function was built into the Shelby console with two metal clips that allowed stowage of the lap belts, eliminating fishing expeditions to retrieve them from under the front seats. The belts were standard black Mustang units that were Shelby-ized with the addition of small "Shelby Cobra" decals on the release buttons.

By 1968, the Mustang fastback had a fixed rear seat as standard equipment with the once-standard folding rear seat as an extra-cost option. All Shelby fastbacks were equipped with the folding seat as one of several "mandatory options" for the model. The rear face of the console contained a courtesy light (the same round unit as in the inner quarter panel) and an ashtray for the rear-seat passengers. A horizontal safety bar was advertised in early promotional literature. Designed to keep luggage from sliding forward off the rear deck in the event of a sudden stop, it was never implemented.

1968 Shelby Mustang GT350, GT500 and GT500 KR
In Detail No. 3

The number of '68 Shelbys factory-equipped with AM-FM Multiplex Stereo radios was in the single digits. It was a fairly pricey option at $170. Air conditioning was much more popular and was fitted to almost a third of the 1968 production.

The only model designation inside the cockpit was the appropriate "GT350" or "GT500" badge (another ACSCO product) mounted on the wood-grained dash above the glove compartment door.

To simplify '68 Shelby production, only one wheel choice was offered from the factory: the Garwood Industries simulated mag wheel cover. The cast-metal center "spider" was engineered to accept the gas cap decal as the center cap emblem, a further simplification of the Shelby build process.

No extant documentation indicates that the Garwood Industries wheel cover was patterned after Pete Brock's '65 Shelby Cragar wheel, but photographic evidence is certainly suggestive.

If the checkered flag fender badges on this red, Garwood-equipped muscle car look more "Chevy" than "Shelby," there's good reason. Garwood wheel covers were offered as options on several bowtie-adorned models, including the Impala and Chevelle. (Photo Courtesy Bob Wilson)

Shelby stylist Charlie McHose never owned an example of the only car he styled solo in 1967, but the next year he traded his '67 Toronado in on a '68 Shelby, which retained a number of his 1967 styling cues. Shortly after he purchased the Acapulco Blue GT500, he decided that the car looked better with plain black wheels than with the fake mag wheels, so the Garwood wheel covers became garage wall art. (Photo Courtesy Charlie McHose)

Although 10-spoke wheels were not available from the factory for 1968, Shelby dealers could (and did) order and install them on a customer's car, for a price, of course. The exception was a half-dozen or so Shelbys, bound for export sales, that rolled out of the Ionia plant shod with the handsome cast-aluminum wheels.

COOKIE-CUTTER CONSISTENCY

Compared to the '67 Shelbys with their myriad running production changes (steel-framed versus all-fiberglass hoods and deck lids, functional versus non-functional brake cooling scoops, braced versus unbraced roll bars, and flat versus curved taillight panels, to name just a few), the 1968 models are often thought to have been produced with absolute and unequivocal commonality, but that's not exactly the case.

Just as with the 1967 build, minor changes by Ford to the platform on which the Shelbys were built serve to differentiate, even if only under careful scrutiny, the early Mustangs from the later ones. Rear seat belt mounting, differences in tachometer lettering, and style of the rear marker lights were some of the almost imperceptible changes implemented as Mustangs marched down Metuchen's assembly line.

A. O. Smith offered the ability to produce the entire run of fiberglass componentry needed for the 1968 build under one roof, unlike any other fiberglass vendor. Even so, the parts were subject to those small along-the-way changes common to almost any production scenario. It can be generalized, however, that the 1968s were, for the most part, as similar to each other as the 1967s were different.

Most, if not all, of the aforementioned changes were of the "running" variety, that is, a change that, once made, is implemented from that point forward with no attempt made to update previously produced articles to the new configuration. However, there were a couple where at least an attempt was made to

1968 Shelby Mustang GT350, GT500 and GT500 KR
In Detail No. 3

retrofit earlier-built cars with a production change. One concerned the GT350's intake manifold. Originally intended to be the 1967-style of aluminum Cobra intake, earlier cars were delivered with as-built Ford cast-iron intakes because when Shelby Cobra Job One rolled off the line, government certification of the aluminum intake wasn't complete.

Owners of cars built with the iron inhalers were notified that when the aluminum articles were ready, they could bring in their cars for an intake swap, but not all bothered. A second change where retrofit was attempted concerned the Marchal fog lights. When Ford realized that the Marchal lights didn't pass government muster, owners of cars delivered with those lights were notified that they could bring them into the selling dealer and have the illegal lights swapped out for approved Lucas units. Again, not all owners took advantage of the offer.

By and large, however, and whether running or otherwise, the production changes that occurred during '68 Shelby production were relatively minor in both scope and number. During the spring of 1968, however, a massive change occurred in the character of big-block Shelbys exiting Ionia.

Early 1968 Shelbys had side-marker lights with a rectangular surround (foreground). Later cars had marker lights with pointed ends (background). The change actually had nothing to do with Shelby production; it was the result of a part changeover on the base Mustang. It's a convenient method to determine, at a glance, whether a '68 Shelby is an early- or late-production car.

A pair of rectangular fog lights was mounted on the lower edge of the upper grille opening. Early cars used Marchal lights (left), but somewhere along the line, someone realized that the "cat's eye" lamps hadn't yet passed government certification, so Lucas lights (right) were substituted and used until the end of 1968 production.

Lower 1968 side scoops were almost identical to 1967 parts in geometry, but unlike 1967 scoops, which evolved from functional to decorative, all 1968 brake scoops were decorative only and lacked functionality (other than as a receptacle for autumn leaves). Two styles of scoops were used, both with very subtle dimensional changes. Later ones (right) had a very pronounced vertical trough between the attaching screws; earlier scoops (left) lacked this depression. There were actually two very slightly different versions of the later style, also the result of mold changes made partway through production.

The '68 GT350s and GT500s used the 1967 GT500 aluminum air-cleaner lid that was designed for a dual-carb application to be secured with two wingnuts, one atop each carburetor. With both 1968 models using a single carburetor, a bracket arrangement inside the air cleaner featured two studs, allowing the lid to be secured with two wingnuts (left). Later cars deleted the bracket and simply had a hole drilled in the center of the air-cleaner top to attach to the single carburetor's stud (right). Unused attachment holes were plugged with press-in steel buttons.

ROGER MILLER, THE COBRA JET AND THE KING OF THE ROAD

In the spring of 1968, big-block Shelbys began rolling out of A. O. Smith with the most significant running production change yet, a new powerplant under the hood: the 428 Cobra Jet. As with many of Ford's high-performance engines, the CJ was developed for initial use on a race-track, but this track was a mere 1,320 feet in length.

At the 1968 NHRA Winternationals in Pomona in February, Ford fielded a

Despite the substantial performance increase yielded by the 428CJ engine, the flanks of GT500 KRs underwent minimal styling changes; only the side stripe designation and a fender badge were changed. (Photo Courtesy Rodney Harrold)

Replacing the GT500's 360-hp Police Interceptor 428 with the 335 hp Cobra Jet 428 (to create the GT500 KR) seemed, on the surface, a step down in the horsepower department but enthusiasts knew full well that the CJ's horsepower rating was only to snooker NHRA officials (and placate insurance companies). The KR kept the GT500's aluminum "Cobra Le Mans" valvecovers, but replaced the aluminum air cleaner with a ram air induction setup that sealed to a hood air plenum. A 735 Holley sat atop a cast-iron Ford intake. (Photo Courtesy Scott Fuller)

By 1968, "ram air" was in vogue and Shelby wasn't about to miss out. A one-piece, molded plenum was bonded to the underside of GT500 KR hoods, connecting the twin air intake "nostrils" to the CJ's circular air cleaner. The twin air inlets of non-KR GT500 and GT350 hoods simply allowed fresh air into the engine compartment.

quintet of Mustang fastbacks, designated the 1968-½ Cobra Jet, powered by the new CJ. Ford underrated the engine considerably (and deliberately) at 335 hp, but few believed the ultra-conservative rating. In fact, there was evidence to suggest that the actual number of ponies produced was as much as 100 higher than advertised. One contemporary automotive publication theorized that the actual number was within putting distance of 500.

The actual horsepower wasn't nearly as important as the fact that as the Winternationals drew to a close, the CJs dominated. At the end of the day, the 428CJ came out on top of the heap (with the final heat being a CJ versus CJ showdown). It was a Ford marketing dream come true.

THE SNAKE IS QUICKER THAN THE BOWTIE

To go along with the more muscular big-block, Shelby wanted a new name for the upgraded model and this culminated in one of the best-known (but also one of the most misunderstood) tales of Carroll Shelby and his cars. As often told by Shelby himself in later years, he had learned of a soon-to-be-released General Motors muscle machine that was to be called the "King of the Road." A quick investigation revealed that General Motors hadn't yet trademarked the designation, so, by the next morning, Shelby Automotive did.

The new model replaced the GT500 in Shelby's two-car lineup, and was called the Cobra GT500 KR, the "King of the Road." It was a matter of beating General Motors to the punch with its own model designation. Despite what has been conjectured since, it had nothing at all to do with country singer Roger Miller's hobo hit recording of the same name from a few years prior.

Appearance changes for the KR were relatively minor. The Cobra Jet's quad exhaust tips (actually a double tip welded to each dual tailpipe) let someone know that they were following a KR-powered Shelby. The gas cap logo (and also wheel cover center) was changed to incorporate the wording "Cobra Jet" in place of "Shelby Cobra." A "Cobra Jet" dash badge (similar in overall shape and size to the "GT350" and "GT500" badges) identified Cobra Jet power to the car's occupants. A unique side stripe

The "King of the Road" had nothing to do with engineers, boxcars, midnight trains to Bangor, or any other aspect of the hobo lifestyle sung about in Roger Miller's country hit of the same name. It was simply a matter of Carroll Shelby claim-jumping on a not-yet-copyrighted name that General Motors planned to use on an upcoming Chevy muscle car. In the fast-paced dog-eat-dog world of 1960s performance car development and marketing, it was the early bird that got the worm (and the side stripe designation).

1968 Shelby Mustang GT350, GT500 and GT500 KR
In Detail No. 3

The longer "G.T.500 KR" designation didn't fit in the side stripe on the bottom of the front fender if rendered in the Shelby standard Microgramma Extended Bold font, so a change to Sans Copperplate Gothic Bold for the new model was implemented. Side stripe lettering on GT350 and GT500 (for the remainder of that model's existence) stayed in Microgramma. Further space was saved by eliminating the periods after the "E" and "T."

An electronic starter delay was installed in all 428-powered Fords after mid-April 1968. It was previously thought that the delay was unique to the 428CJ engine, but the delay was actually installed on all 1968 Ford 428-powered cars. The remedy was more troublesome than the malady it was intended to cure and the finicky device was discontinued in 1969.

OPPOSITE TOP LEFT: The GT500 KR used the entire Cobra Jet Mustang's exhaust system, including the quad exhaust pipe tips. The smaller-diameter CJ tailpipes featured a rolled-in edge to the outlets, in place of the sharp-edged Shelby tailpipes.

OPPOSITE, TOP RIGHT: To identify the more powerful KR, a slight variation was made to the gas cap and wheel center cap emblem; the graphics were left unchanged, but the words "Shelby Cobra" were replaced with "Cobra Jet."

OPPOSITE, BOTTOM LEFT: GT500 KRs with automatic transmissions were outfitted with a unique wood shift handle with a silver inlaid snake. Designed and fabricated by ACSCO Products, the handle was made by snipping the coiled snake from Cobra keychains, bending it over a piece of pipe to give it the correct curvature, then epoxying the shake into a recess in the wooden shift handle. Manual-transmission KRs used the standard Shelby white and blue shift knob.

OPPOSITE, BOTTOM RIGHT: King of the Road models sported a unique dash badge, a restyling of the GT350/500 emblem: the coiled "S" snake now appeared in gold, and upright "Cobra Jet" lettering replaced the other model's italicized "GT350" or "GT500" text.

LEFT: The original intent was for the GT500 KR to replace the GT500, but dealers hadn't sold the 500s before the newer KRs started showing up. It was therefore possible, for some period of time, to choose between either model in stock at dealers.

In addition to the side stripe designation, GT500 KR cars were identified by a "428 Cobra Jet" emblem alongside the fender-mounted coiled-snake badge. Also created by ACSCO Products, it replaced the "Cobra" badge below the snake emblem (which was used on non-Cobra Jet cars).

incorporating the "GT500 KR" model designation was designed and finally, the "Cobra" emblem under the coiled-snake fender ornament was replaced with a "428 Cobra Jet" badge.

As with many of Shelby's change-over products, there was no last GT500 followed immediately by the first GT500 KR; the two were actually built simultaneously for a short time as GT500 parts were exhausted. Because of this intermingled nature of GT500 and GT500 KR production, GT500s were built (or "completed") after KR production began. A good bit of May was already history when KR production began and it continued throughout the remainder of '68 Shelby production at A. O. Smith. The availability of a 428 in a Mustang (as opposed to previously only in a Shelby Mustang) was one of the first steps in the dilution of Shelby exclusivity.

Shelby GT500s, previously at the top of the line and having only the ultimate in performance goodies, now shared their powerplants with Cobra Jet Mustangs, which actually came first. Further in-house competition came from the Mach I and Boss Mustangs the next year. Shelby's loss of exclusivity in the Ford performance arena just added fuel to the fire for Carroll, who wanted to call it quits.

GOLD (NON) STANDARD

One problem is related to the KR if only by a coincidence in timing. After the very first Sunlit Gold Mustang was unloaded from the railcar in Ionia, the stunning color became a thorn that embedded itself deeper and deeper into the backside of A. O. Smith. As almost any body and paint technician can attest, silvers and golds are particularly susceptible to showing great differences in appearance as a result of the application process. The cars rolling out of the Metuchen assembly plant were no exception. But in all fairness to Metuchen, they were likely no better or no worse in terms of consistency than gold cars emanating from any of Ford's other assembly plants.

All of the Shelby fiberglass add-on parts were pre-painted before installation, and often before the arrival of the actual cars themselves. Therefore, the gold hoods, deck lids, noses, and side scoops didn't match the gold cars on which they were to be installed, which created a tremendous headache for A. O. Smith. After voicing several complaints to Shelby Automotive and, in turn, to Ford, a Ford representative confirmed that the gold cars he inspected at Smith's facility did indeed differ from the specification for that color. The problem worsened, and even resulted in Smith having to disassemble 38 already-completed gold cars and repaint the fiberglass parts with a special mix of gold that matched not the standard for Sunlit Gold, but rather, the off-color cars themselves.

Smith's MacFarlane and Shelby's Kerr went back and forth on the issue of responsibility, never really reaching agreement on anything other than the replacement of Sunlit Gold with a yellow culled from the Ford fleet color catalog. This yellow, identified only as WT 6066, replaced Sunlit Gold just after big-block Shelby production at Metuchen had

Although Sunlit Gold may have been popular with Shelby owners, it wasn't with A. O. Smith, which discovered that its gold pre-painted Shelby parts didn't match the gold Mustangs on which they were installed. The Metuchen cars featured a wide range of shade variations from the specification Sunlit Gold. After the disassembly, repaint, and reassembly of more than three dozen completed cars was necessary, Shelby and Ford agreed that no more gold cars would leave Metuchen bound for Ionia. Another, less troublesome color was substituted.

switched over to the KR model. Thus, there are no Sunlit Gold GT500 KRs just as there are no WT 6066 GT500s. In total, 143 Shelbys (the plan was for 144 WT 6066 cars but a production error resulted in 1 fewer), both GT350 and GT500 KR, fastback and convertible, wore WT 6066. Shelby Automotive released a unique set of black "GT350" and "GT500 KR" side stripes for use on those yellow cars only.

WT 6066 reappeared on the '70 Mustang color charts as "Bright Yellow" and was humorously named "Last Stand Custard" when sprayed onto the new Maverick.

TOP: For A. O. Smith, WT 6066 yellow was like a breath of fresh air. The problems of off-color gold cars coming in from Metuchen were (thankfully) a thing of the past. WT 6066 re-emerged on the '70 Mustang color charts as "Bright Yellow" and was humorously applied to '70 Mavericks as "Last Stand Custard." Both carried Ford color code "D." (Photo Courtesy J. D. Kaltenbach)

BOTTOM: A special black side stripe was devised for use on WT 6066 yellow GT350s and GT500 KRs (by the time yellow was substituted for Sunlit Gold, GT500 production had ended). All other color 350s and KRs received white side stripes; Wimbledon White cars were striped in blue. Of the six total special paint colors, WT 6066 yellow was the only color applied to convertibles as well as fastback Shelbys. (Photo Courtesy Scott Fuller)

A handful of just-completed Shelby Cobras await shipment out of A. O. Smith to Shelby dealers nationwide in late summer of 1968, near the end of that year's Shelby production. The GT500 KR and WT 6066 yellow have become synonymous over the years although there is less exclusivity to the pair than is often believed. Of the 1,571 GT500 KRs built, only 129 were yellow and of the 143 yellow Shelbys, not all were KRs; 14 were GT350s. (Photo Courtesy Jack Redeker)

MORE COLOR CURIOSITIES

At about the same time that WT 6066 showed up, 15 other Shelbys (in both fastback GT350 and GT500 KR form) were scheduled to arrive in five other colors (three cars of each color), also pulled from the fleet catalog. Little documentation exists about why these 15 cars were built. Some, but not all, were sold during a summer sales contest that ran from May through October 1968. The five special colors, known by only a color number, are WT 4017 red, WT 7081 green, WT 5185 orange, WT 5014 orange, and WT 5107 orange.

Like WT 6066 yellow, these special colors came into existence after production had changed over to the GT500 KR, so there are no GT500s to which any of the special colors have been applied.

The "tradition" of unique Shelby design features sometimes carried over onto the base Mustang line a year or so later also held for some of the colors: WT 5185 orange became Calypso Coral, which was available on Boss Mustangs in 1969 ('69 Shelbys so painted were said to be done in Competition Orange), and WT 5014 orange became Grabber Orange, which was offered in 1970.

As is often the Shelby case, the plan and the execution didn't always jive and the special-paint cars were no exception. The original plan of three cars of five colors became four cars each of WT 7081 green and WT 5107 orange but only two cars each of WT 5014 orange and WT 4017 red. Only the group of WT 5185 orange cars contained the correct three vehicles.

Just as the six special colors are an unusual aspect of otherwise very uniform '68 Shelby production, the prescribed means for an owner to identify those colors for the purpose of paint repair was equally unorthodox. On these 15 special-paint cars, the space normally filled with the Ford color code letter on the car's door ID tag was left blank, leaving the owner of one of these special-color cars with no idea how to obtain touch-up paint.

Executives at Ford had thought of this eventuality and the subject was covered in a memo that was distributed to the selling dealers of all '68 Shelbys. In the case of a missing color code on the door tag, the memo instructed the owner to request that the dealer obtain, from Ford and at a cost of $5 per copy, a fleet color chip catalog. The memo

WT 7081 green was one of five special paint colors applied to a very small quantity of '68 Shelbys. The originally scheduled application to a threesome of cars shifted slightly due to production mix-ups. The final result was four green cars: two GT350s, and two GT500 KRs. Unlike WT 6066 yellow, which found its way onto fastbacks as well as convertibles, all of the other five special colors were applied to fastbacks only, but in a mix of small- and big-block cars. (Photo Courtesy Mike Tillery)

If there was something a bit déjà vu about WT 5185 orange, it was because it had a previous life. It had been applied to some 1964½ Mustangs as Poppy Red (Ford color code "3"). It re-emerged in 1969 as Calypso Coral (also color code "3"), but when applied to '69 Cougars and Shelbys, it was called Competition Orange (it was also named Flower Power Red, one of two applied to the 1969 Mustang Limited Edition 600, built as a sales promotion for the Philadelphia district). WT 5185 was the only one of the five special paints to end up being applied in the planned quantity of three cars, a single GT350 and a pair of GT500 KRs. (Photo Courtesy Colin Comer)

Because of a production error, the planned trio of WT 5014 orange fastbacks ended up as a pair, a GT350 and a GT500 KR. The color resurfaced in 1969 on the Shelby color charts, picking up the name Grabber Orange (Ford color code "U"), and became available on Mustangs in 1970. It was called Competition Gold when applied to a Cougar. (Photo Courtesy Fred Warf)

instructed the dealer to determine, visually, the color of the Shelby compared to the color chips, which carried the designation on the reverse side. That identified the special color by its "WT" number. The memo also cross-referenced the special color with various paint suppliers' (DuPont, Ditzler, R&M) product numbers.

What no one apparently realized when developing that somewhat convoluted process of paint code determination is that each of those special-color cars had the "WT" color number stamped onto the fender body buck tag.

A REDUCED RENT-A-RACER REVIVAL

It was likely that before Hertz even received the final installment of its 1,000 exclusive 1966 Shelby GT350Hs that the rental company began to realize that the '66 Shelby wasn't the car for them. Shelby built sports cars, but Hertz wanted sporty cars; cars that looked the part, but were easy to operate. The GT350, with bicep-building manual steering and both-feet-required manual brakes may have been the 1965 SCCA B-Production National Champion, but it was definitely not easy to operate. Before that realization

Removing the "bang-and-clunk" Detroit Locker differential, adding a rear seat and an automatic transmission, and making them available in a rainbow of color schemes did little to soften the '66 GT350 enough to satisfy Hertz's broad spectrum of client driver abilities and preferences. Hertz's maintenance people were also unprepared for the care and feeding of high-performance machinery.

The 1968 Shelby Cobra in Detail: The Same . . . But Different
Chapter 4

The company that put you in the driver's seat opted out of a special "Hertz-only" convertible when the idea was pitched in 1967 (for a 1968 model). Forty years later, the rental car company bought in with a fleet of 500 2007 black-and-gold Shelby GT-H (for "Hertz") convertibles as an encore to its 500 very-well-received '06 GT-H coupes. The source of inspiration for a color scheme was a no-brainer.

set in at Hertz, there was talk of an additional 1966 cars and as many as 2,000 1967 GT350H units, but both purchases were eventually zeroed out.

Shelby didn't give up completely on the idea of a Hertz-unique model with the demise of the planned '67 GT350H. It made one more attempt at a special rental Shelby in November of that year. A pitch to Hertz for a Hertz-only Shelby convertible didn't bear fruit (although hopefulness manifested itself in the inclusion of gold GT350H side striping in an early version of the '68 Shelby parts list). Although the rental company opted out of a fleet of just-for-Hertz Shelby convertibles, it didn't turn its back on Shelby Automotive completely.

MORE APPROPRIATE FOR THE MASSES

The Hertz/Shelby partnership wasn't dead; it was just undergoing an adjust-

ment. After a one-model-year hiatus, 1968 marked the return of the Shelby GT350 to the ranks of the Hertz Sports Car Club. But the 1968 version of the "rent-a-racer" was a much different animal than the one offered to the car-renting public in 1966. Across the board, the '68 Shelby was a much tamer version of the modified Mustang than the 1966 car. While some lamented the toning-down of the GT350's performance, the fact that it was a very different car is precisely what reignited Hertz's enthusiasm.

There is little argument that the '68 Shelbys had become more refined than the earlier models, and by Hertz's own admission, this refinement made them more to the company's (and their clientele's) liking. To be successful, Hertz had to satisfy the needs of a large cross-section of the driving public. They needed the look, but not necessarily the feel, of something sporty. Renters wanted the rewards of driving what they considered a "sports car" without having to put forth the effort usually associated with them.

The cars that Hertz made available in 1968 through its Sports Car Club no longer appealed to only a narrow band of performance car enthusiasts. The new Shelby was attractive and acceptable to a broader segment of clientele.

The new Shelby seemed to fit the rental car company's needs perfectly. In February and March that year, Hertz took delivery of approximately 230 (production records lack completeness) of the new, refined "rent-a-racers," marketed under the tagline "rent a car your wife may never let you own."

Unlike the special edition GT350H of 1966, the 1968 Hertz models were standard Shelby Cobra GT350 fastbacks. They were almost identically equipped with automatic transmission, power disc brakes,

power steering, tinted glass, shoulder harness, fold-down rear seat, push-button AM radio, and most had air conditioning. The Hertz cars came primarily from three separate DSOs (one of the three DSOs contained non–air conditioned cars). Some non-rental cars were also intermingled in the build, which further highlights that the '68 Shelbys destined for Hertz were indistinguishable from dealer cars. As such, the Hertz cars were delivered in the standard Shelby colors available for 1968 and, like their non-rental brethren, all wore wheel covers.

After the bitter aftertaste of its '66 Shelby experience, Hertz awaited the return of the right type of vehicle for its clientele. When the 1968 Shelby Cobra GTs debuted, they found the kind of cars that they actually needed all along, even if they were not Carroll Shelby's kind of cars.

Hertz toyed with a purchase of '67 Shelbys for its fleet but ultimately decided the car was still too rough for the average driver. A year later, however, Hertz found that the '68 Shelby Cobra had become a perfect compromise, offering sporty looks and decent performance in a car that could be driven by anyone on city streets. All of Hertz's "for rent" '68 Shelbys were GT350 fastbacks, delivered in the standard range of Shelby colors. (There was no special "Hertz" edition as there was in 1966.)

A SHELBY COBRA HARDTOP (SORT OF)

Ford Motor Company's practice of crushing prototype vehicles was followed, and "Little Red," the influence for the California Special Mustang, fell victim to that mandate in the 1970s. Thankfully, the snappy, red notchback continues to live on thanks to a reproduction created by NorCal Motorsports of Sacramento. (Photo Courtesy NorCal Motorsports)

Serious consideration was given to expanding the Shelby Mustang line to include the Model 65 hardtop body style for some time before a hardtop '67 Mustang was delivered to Shelby American in November 1966. This car was one of a trio of Candy Apple Red hardtop/convertible/fastback big-block cars.

The notchback was completed with full '67 Shelby bodywork (and with a black vinyl roof) in early December as a combination "engine/powertrain/whatever else was on Shelby's mind at the time" test bed for a proposed notchback Shelby Mustang. Because of its bright red color, it was quickly was given the nickname of "Little Red" by Shelby American's chief engineer Fred Goodell. He, equally quickly, snatched up the spiffy red hardtop as his daily driver.

The car's nickname proved to be a bit of a misnomer because there was far from anything "little" about the red coupe's performance. Powered by a supercharged 427 and later a blown 428 (with both manual and automatic transmissions), the car's constant tire-chirping was the perfect example of one of Shelby's favorite adages: "too much is just enough."

The car was shown publicly at the 1967 Los Angeles Auto Show in January to considerable enthusiasm and seemed to foretell of a three-car Shelby Mustang product line. The idea of a Shelby notchback still existed in May, when A. O. Smith first submitted its price quotation to Shelby and Ford for GT350/GT500 production. The idea continued to exist in June, when the quote was updated. Shelby Mustangs began rolling out the doors of the A. O. Smith facility in Ionia in November. However, nary a notchback was seen anywhere. But that doesn't mean that there wasn't someplace where a hardtop Mustang with Shelby styling was produced; it just wasn't at A. O. Smith and it wasn't a Shelby. Well, not exactly.

CAMARO, FIREBIRD AND JAVELIN MADE IT HAPPEN

In the spring of 1967, Lee Grey, the Los Angeles district sales manager, visited Shelby American to seek ideas to remedy the Mustang's slumping sales. When the Mustang debuted in 1964 and created a whole new class of automobile, it was the only game in town. There were no other contenders in the pony car arena and it was at the top of the heap. But by the end of the 1967 model year, the pony car class was (or would very soon be) occupied by all manner of new or redesigned long-hood/short-deck lid sporty cars with names including Camaro, Firebird, Javelin, and Barracuda.

Just as the Mustang established the pony car class of automobiles, it was Mustang that showed that when you are at the top, there is only one way to go. Individually, none of Mustang's contenders had anywhere near the sales clout to be serious threats, but in numbers there is strength and, collectively, the other guys began to nibble away at Mustang sales. Even sibling Cougar contributed to the downturn.

When he arrived at Shelby American, Lee spotted "Little Red" and asked Carroll if he could borrow the car for a while. For the next two weeks, Grey drove the car all around the Los Angeles area, showing it off to dealers and any other Ford executive he could find. His plan, maturing every day he had "Little Red," was to create a regional Mustang, a Shelby-influenced Mustang exclusively for the Southern California market. The idea had merit on several fronts: it made sense

stylistically because Los Angeles was, after all, the epicenter of the Shelby universe. It also made sense fiscally; throughout the 1960s, Grey's Los Angeles district accounted for very consistently nearly a full fifth of Ford's nationwide sales.

Grey made sure that the flashy red coupe was in a prominent spot in the parking lot of the Century Plaza Hotel in Beverly Hills in the middle of summer when Ford dealers were holding their annual sales meeting. During the meeting, Grey showed the red coupe to guest speaker Ford Motor Company Vice President Lee Iacocca and pitched the idea of a special edition hardtop Mustang for the Southern California region. Iacocca, who was also a strong proponent of "regionalized" vehicles, wholeheartedly concurred. The concept of the Mustang California Special had just taken its first step toward becoming reality.

CS (BUT NOT FOR CARROLL SHELBY)

Iacocca returned to Dearborn armed with photos of "Little Red"; the actual vehicle was shipped to Dearborn shortly thereafter. By September, just a few short weeks after Iacocca was first shown the red notchback, Ford styling created a Shelby-influenced hardtop Mustang. It was, in essence, a simplified version of the Shelby prototype. Using '68 Shelby componentry (already in production at A. O. Smith) for the car's tail, two hardtop concepts were rendered, with one concept rendered on each side of a production '67 Mustang coupe. The nose of the concept hardtop retained its stock Mustang hood

A Shelby Cobra Hardtop (sort of)
Chapter 5

and grille, to keep costs in check.

The concepts were called the Mustang 350 and one featured a wide body-side "C" stripe enveloping the number "350." The selection of that number was no random grab. Ford marketing people envisioned pitching the creation as a "low-cost Shelby," one that was affordable to anyone. Although this might seem to be a dilution of the Shelby line's exclusivity, Ford management was far less interested in Shelby's status than they were in Ford's car sales.

The other side had a single, constant-width, mid-door-height stripe that ended just aft of the side scoop. The stripe on the side scoop contained cutout lettering that allowed the body-colored "350" to show through; the designation was soon changed to GT/SC, which stood for GT Sport Coupe.

The styling of both concepts was exactly what Lee Grey had in mind, although Ford's marketing folks had a better, or at least, a very different, idea. They proposed marketing the 350 (or the "SC") not just to Southern California, as Grey envisioned, but to the whole country.

The debate persisted for several weeks, but in October 1967, Grey and Iacocca prevailed and the regional Mustang project was given the go-ahead. Grey did have to make one small concession, but it was an altogether palatable one: in order to justify marketing costs, the California Special was available for the northern California (San Jose) district as well. Although it was no longer a Southern California Mustang exclusively, it was still a Mustang exclusively for California.

The stripe graphic chosen for production was the constant-width version but the lettering on the side scoop was reversed and now read "GT/CS," the CS standing for California Special. The Mustang California Special was marketed under the tag line "California Made It Happen," but it was a combination of the Mustang's competition, Lee Grey's vision, Lee Iacocca's perseverance, and, of course, the Shelby Cobra GT's styling, that all conspired to make it happen.

BUILT FOR CALIFORNIA, IN CALIFORNIA

Toward the end of October, A. O. Smith submitted its cost proposal to Shelby Automotive and Ford for GT/CS production, but it was a different approach than was used for building the Shelby Mustangs. Because the California Special was for the California market, it made the most logistical sense to manufacture the cars in that state, to minimize transportation and distribution costs.

Beginning in December, A. O. Smith manufactured, primed, and wet-sanded 700 sets monthly of Shelby components to be used in California Special production. The paint-ready parts were then packed and shipped to Ford's San Jose assembly plant, where actual GT/CS production took place. This was the first time that fiberglass components were installed on a production line vehicle by San Jose.

To ensure a smooth installation onto the hardtops, Smith sent a representative to oversee the first cars' production. In one respect, production of the California

Specials at San Jose was done the way Shelby production in Ionia should have been done, with the fiberglass parts painted side-by-side with the bodies onto which they were to be installed. As a result, color match issues on the California Special build were virtually nonexistent and even GT/CS cars painted in Sunlit Gold (unlike their Shelby cousins) were assembled without difficulty.

In late November, as the Smith-San Jose interaction was being finalized and actual component production was ready to begin, two prototype/promotional California Special hardtops were constructed. By December, right on schedule, A. O. Smith began shipping wrapped, boxed, and palleted fiberglass parts to San Jose. On January 18, 1968, production of the Mustang GT California Special began.

On the day after Valentine's Day approximately 200 cars had been completed but not yet released to dealers. A handful of production California Specials were revealed at festivities held that day, appropriately, at the Century Plaza Hotel. At the end of the gala evening event, emceed by Grey, Los Angeles district dealers had placed more than 1,000 orders for the cars.

A week later, in the San Jose district, a similar unveiling was held. At the beginning of March, official advertising of the GT/CS began in local California newspapers, on television, and on the radio.

By all accounts, production at San Jose went off without a hitch, or at least with relatively few hitches. But back at A. O. Smith in Ionia, issues unrelated to production but rather to cost began to

surface. When the plastics firm bid the California Special project, it did so with the assumption that all the components used on the GT/CS would have been the already-released Shelby GT350/GT500 parts. No engineering would have been involved, just part production, packing, and shipping. But right from the start, Smith was asked to perform engineering that it hadn't included in its bid. The primary perpetrators were developing patterns and methodology to cut openings in the metal Mustang hood for the twist locks, developing mounting for the fog lights in the stock Mustang grille, and redesigning the side scoops to accept grilles in the openings.

Just as with the Shelby Cobra production effort, when additional cost issues cropped up, Smith simply kept working and tallied up the costs, but it was months

Although the rear components (taillights, taillight panel, spoilered deck lid, and quarter-panel extensions) for the California Special were Shelby Cobra production items, a different paint treatment yielded a completely different look. The double trim stripe around the top edge of the rear spoiler found its way onto the stern of the '69 Mustang Mach I. (Photo Courtesy Tom Clark)

after the last Cobra rolled off the line that the California Special cost issues were settled, and not to anywhere near the complete satisfaction of A. O. Smith.

Despite considerable enthusiasm from Ford, customer response to the Shelby-ized California Special fell short of expectations and in late March/early April, the decision was made to extend CS marketing and availability into the Salt Lake City, Seattle, Phoenix, Vancouver, and Calgary districts as well. CS availability in the Oklahoma City, Dallas, and Houston district also followed.

At the end of July, production of a second "regional" Mustang kicked off. It was marketed as the High Country

A week after the Los Angeles district was introduced to the Mustang GT/California Special, a similar gala reveal was held for the Golden State's northern district (San Jose) at San Francisco's Fairmount Hotel. (Photo Courtesy Paul M. Newitt)

Engineering involved in adapting the driving lights to the grille, the twist locks to the steel Mustang hood, and grilles into the side scoops was something not anticipated by A. O. Smith when it bid on the California Special project. Those additional costs contributed to cost overruns in what should have been a simple production effort for Smith. (Photo Courtesy Rodney Harrold)

Several examples of Shelby styling cues found their way onto Mustangs of later years. One example of reciprocity was the striping of the GT/CS the mid-door-height side stripe (complete with body-colored-show-through lettering) that reappeared on the flanks of the '69 and '70 Shelby GT350 and GT500.

Special (HCS) for the Denver district. The HCS was essentially a standard GT/CS trim package but with a triangular High Country Special decal on the side scoops, in place of the GT/CS lettering. The quarter-panel "California Special" script was also deleted.

The 251 High Country Mustangs produced brought the total California Special production to 4,118 cars, which was somewhat short of Ford's initial plan for 5,500 units, and just 10 percent below eventual GT350 and GT500 production. Production of the GT/CS ended on July 18, six months to the day after it began at San Jose.

The Mustang California Special was an interesting (almost paradoxical) series of "was" and "was nots." First and foremost, it was not a Shelby. But it was Shelby-related, using components manufactured side-by-side with parts destined for the Shelby GT350s and GT500s. It was also Shelby-influenced, borrowing its styling cues from a genuine prototype Shelby Mustang. And finally, it was as close to

a production manifestation of a Shelby notchback as there ever would be. These characteristics make the California Special not a Shelby, but a very close and often overlooked relative.

Neither Shelby's vision of a hardtop companion to the Cobra fastbacks and convertibles, nor Ford's of a low-cost hardtop Mustang with Shelby styling came to complete fruition. The Mustang GT/California Special (and its companion High Country Special) were the embodiment of parts of both concepts. (Photo Courtesy Rich DiMarino)

CHAPTER 6

LEGACY AND LEGEND

It was never the intent of Shelby Automobiles to offer top stripes as a 1968 factory option, but some owners (even those of relatively new cars) decided that "Shelby" and "stripes" were synonymous. Because the factory wouldn't apply them, they took matters into their own hands and painted them on themselves. Today, the stripes are gradually disappearing as cars are returned to original specifications; even wheel covers are making a limited comeback.

For years, the 1968 Shelby had been regarded somewhat as the illegitimate stepchild of Carroll's family of Mustangs, never having achieved acceptance on a par with that of the earlier California ponies. With minimal extant historical paperwork shedding equally minimal light on the design and build process, it had long been believed that these were failed attempts at creating vehicles identical to Shelby's earlier creations and that the '68 Cobra GT was, in fact, a shot that far missed its intended mark.

In recent years, however, factory documentation on the 1968 models has begun to surface, and what has turned up shows that these were not cars that "just happened"; neither were they examples of requirements aimed for but ultimately unfulfilled. They were cars that were specifically designed for a Shelby clientele very different from earlier buyers.

The '68 Shelby evolved into less of a performance and more of a luxury car. That evolution was part of a deliberate and well-thought-out design process that was implemented to maintain relevance of the Shelby Mustangs. As more factory paperwork reveals itself, it becomes apparent that the 1968 GT350, GT500, and GT500 KR happened exactly the way they were intended to.

EXPLAINING (OR TRYING TO) THE UNEXPLAINABLE

Based on a litany of criteria, there is little argument that the '68 Shelby is

It is not their lack of performance compared to contemporary automobiles, but rather their values, that render '68 Shelbys impractical for use as daily drivers.

a desirable automobile, but the question of what makes it so is one not easily answered. Certainly one component (although by no means the only one) of desirability is rarity. Generally speaking, the more limited the production quantity of a given automobile, the greater its desirability. At first glance, the '68 Shelby Cobra seems to be anything but limited with almost eight times as many produced as the first year of the GT350 and in excess of 1,000 more than either the preceding or succeeding years. The 1968 edition of Mr. Shelby's Mustang falls within a cat's whisker of making up a full third of the total production of all years of the marque; none of that sounds like rarity.

But in the context of a comparison to a wider production base of automobiles, the '68 Shelby's rarity begins to stand out: 317,404 '68 Mustangs were produced, of

which a mere 4,450 became Shelby Cobra GTs. If that sounds like artificially skewing the argument because of the Mustang's enormous production totals, consider a comparison to the '68 Shelby's primary competition (according to Shelby): the Pontiac GTO. In this case, the numbers are GTO, 87,684; Shelby, 4,450. It is still insignificant by comparison.

So, it is a fair assessment that the '68 Shelby is a rare automobile? Rarity is an objective thing. Production numbers answer the question with little guesswork or theorizing. And, other ingredients are in the desirability concoction that are not as easy to understand or explain.

One factor that certainly contributes to the '68 Shelby's desirability is not what separates it from other 1960s muscle cars but one that makes them very much alike: the state of American automotive

1968 Shelby Mustang GT350, GT500 and GT500 KR
In Detail No. 3

Not an explanation, but certainly an indication of the '68 Shelby's desirability is their pampered treatment at car shows and other automotive events today.

development in the 1960s. Cars of the 1960s, while perhaps viewed as primitive by today's computer-equipped examples, had actually reached a level of technological sophistication unlike cars of any previous generation. Back then, Throttle Position Sensor was simply another term for the driver's right foot.

The best explanation of this is an example. Nearly a half-century after their birth, '68 Shelbys are just as drivable on contemporary roads as they were then. And, in all fairness, so are their kin from the same period. This is something that cannot be said for a 1910 Model T, for example, cruising the interstate in 1960, 50 years after its birth, trying in vain to keep pace with a 375 hp Chrysler 300F.

Two components of desirability (rarity and drivability) have thus far been identified, they have a definite lack of completeness, for there are many automobiles that possess those two qualities but are not considered desirable. There is more to the equation and perhaps a good source for the balance may be a collection of words and their definitions; that is, the dictionary.

Hopes for finding a simple, concise explanation of what makes the '68 Shelby desirable in the dictionary, however, are somewhat dashed. Although Webster does offer a few definitions, those definitions possess a decided lack of specificity. "Desirable" is explained as having good

or pleasing qualities and worth having or acquiring. The attributes are clearly listed, but not so clearly explained. For example, just what constitutes "pleasing qualities," or "worth having"?

With a dictionary definition falling short, it may well be that a concise definition of "desirable" is just as elusive as Justice Potter Stewart's definition of pornography: He can't explain it, but he knows it when he sees it. It is perhaps best to abandon the quest for an itemized, absolute explanation of desirable and simply agree that the '68 Shelby's style, performance, rarity, and drivability conspire to make it a desirable 1960s automobile.

AFFORDABILITY BEGETS UNAFFORDABILITY

Of the entire family of Shelby Mustangs built between 1965 and 1970, the 1968 cars have, traditionally, occupied the "most affordable" slot in the price hierarchy. But an interesting phenomenon (not unique to Shelbys) is occurring, one that is changing the price dynamic of the Shelby Mustang hierarchy. Simply put, but seeming counterintuitive, it is that current affordability creates future unaffordability, an illustrative example being the Ferrari 206/246 Dino.

Derided from its inception as being "not a true Ferrari" and "nothing more than a rebadged Fiat," the handsome Dinos, for the longest time, occupied the lowest price slot in the Ferrari value structure. However, as the prices of other, higher-dollar (and more accepted) Ferraris skyrocketed out of sight, the 206/246 series began to experience an upsurge in popularity, largely due to their affordability.

That popularity drove the prices higher and higher and also boosted their

Convertibles are at the upper end of desirability for each model (GT350, GT500, and GT500 KR). Convertibles with options such as air conditioning bump it up a notch. Air-conditioned GT500 KR convertibles are perhaps at the top of the '68 Shelby desirability food chain. (Photo Courtesy Scott Fuller)

acceptability within the Ferrari community. Soon, Dinos were commanding well into six figures, ironically putting them out of the reach of the very enthusiasts who instigated their popularity upswing. An additional price upsurge was created by collectors and investors who, upon seeing (or sensing) the increase in desirability of the Dinos, started snatching them up as well, creating an additional shortage in supply, further escalating the prices.

The same phenomenon is occurring with the '68 Shelbys as the values of early cars (the California-built 1965, 1966, and 1967 models) climb out of reach of most enthusiasts. This casts the '68 GT350 and GT500 in a new light. The A. O. Smith-constructed Mustangs are enjoying an increase in popularity, desirability, collectability, and value.

THE PRICE PYRAMID

One way to guarantee the obsolescence of any publication on the subject of any group of collector automobiles (although the phenomenon is not limited to wheeled things) is to present a listing of the current value of those automobiles. The collector car market (of which muscle cars are certainly a subset) is subject to both seasonal influences and "other global factors." As soon as whatever words on the subject are put to paper, that analysis has been rendered obsolete by a change in the very same market conditions that are being analyzed; things change that fast.

The '68 Shelby Cobra is no different from any other muscle car in this respect,

but one aspect of the value discussion that has, over the past several years, remained relatively constant, is the value hierarchy of the different models, body styles, and features. Pricing of the '68 Shelbys follows a relatively simple and logical hierarchy: within the same body style, big-blocks command higher prices than small-blocks and in a given engine displacement, convertibles fetch more than do fastbacks.

Intermingling the two variables of engine size and body style, the price/value points, from lowest to highest, are: GT350 fastback, GT350 convertible, GT500 fastback, GT500 convertible, GT500 KR fastback, and GT500 KR convertible. But there are caveats. Because of their low production totals, GT350 convertibles are very much on par with, and in many instances, command higher prices than the next step up, the GT500 fastbacks. In many instances, there is a substantial gap between GT500 KR fastbacks and convertibles; the relatively rare air-conditioned GT500 KR convertibles run away from the fastbacks in terms of prices.

EXTRAORDINARY WITHIN THE MUNDANE

Although the '68 Shelby Cobra is thought of as being built with total and unequivocal uniformity, "unique" is a word that isn't often associated with it, but it is "atypical" nestled among the typical, if you look in the right place.

One group that meets the criteria of uniqueness is the handful of cars built with special paint. With only 15 cars in this fraternity, you cannot argue their rarity and even if you add larger quantity of yellow cars, the special paint group expands to a mere 158 (which, out of 4,450 total, is still a miniscule number).

The unusual colors are not for everyone, but those who fancy them are truly passionate about their machines. One collector who, after purchasing a yellow, air-conditioned GT500 KR convertible, learned that there were only three other identical cars produced, spent several years searching for those elusive machines to add to his collection (which he eventually did). Values of the lowest-priced GT350 fastbacks inch upward by the application of special paint and also push up the values of GT500 KRs on which they were applied.

The approximately 230 GT350 fastbacks acquired by Hertz is another group of cars that have their values enhanced by a bit of unusual history. Although these cars are not special Hertz models as they were in 1966, the much-understated (by comparison) 1968 rental cars nonetheless have a unique place in the Shelby story and their ex-rental status helps increase their values a bit, compared to other GT350s.

THE NUMBERS GAME

As with the earlier Shelbys built in California (and in fact, something true of virtually all collector cars), provenance and "the numbers" are all-important. The '68 Shelbys are the most "serialized" of all years of the marque, with the Ford VIN of the platform Mustang appearing

With extremely low production totals, the special-paint '68 Shelbys certainly meet the definition of "rare." Although the unique paint isn't everyone's cup of tea, the cars have attracted a following and are real attention-getters at car shows.

True gems in the '68 Shelby world (and the collector car universe in general) are the original paint, original interior "survivor" cars that show exactly how the cars were assembled and painted back in the day. The patina (and an occasional touched-up scuff or ding) of half-century-old paint, which is almost impossible to duplicate, pretty much guarantees that these cars are genuine, and not skillful recreations. (Photo Courtesy Tony Conover)

in no fewer than four places. The Shelby serial number appears on the fender tag. Because the Ford VIN is also part of the Shelby serial number, the correlation between the two is plainly visible on the Shelby tag. The Ford VIN on the Shelby tag also correlates to the Ford VIN in other locations. As long as all the numbers match, you are guaranteed the authenticity and legitimacy of a particular vehicle, right?

Not so fast, for that's a conclusion that can have disastrous consequences. Preliminary examination of a Shelby's VIN is only the first step in the validation and authentication process of a vehicle. It is something that may be thought of as more of a journey than a destination. A given Shelby with all of its appropriate

identification tags with serial numbers on them is that first step.

The next step (verifying that a particular vehicle in question has the *correct* numbers on its tags) requires a call for backup.

TRUST . . . BUT VERIFY

The Shelby American Automobile Club (saac.com), known within the collector vehicle community as simply "SAAC"), has been recognized since its founding in 1975 as the undisputed authority on the history and legacy of all Shelby automobiles. SAAC maintains the SAAC World Registry, a database of all the vehicles produced by Carroll Shelby and his companies from 1962 through 1970. SAAC

1968 Shelby Mustang GT350, GT500 and GT500 KR
In Detail No. 3

also consists of a group of registrars, historians, and experts who are well-versed on specific-year Shelby automobiles and who maintain, in addition to the registry database, collections of original factory documentation that substantiate whether or not the numbers on a given car's ID tags are correct.

The registry database can shed light on a car's history and can indicate if there has been any documented "funny business" (such as other cars with the same serial numbers or large gaps in a car's ownership chain) associated with that particular vehicle.

After a vehicle has been determined to be "all correct," the final step in the validation process includes one of SAAC's concours judges physically inspecting the car. This examination takes into account factors such as the correct date codes on integral structural members (such as welded-in rocker panels), and also verifies construction details such as that the welds appear to be factory- and period-correct.

Confirmation of a car's pedigree and authenticity becomes increasingly important as the values of Shelby automobiles climb well into the six-figure

Not all '68 Shelbys, however, have aged gracefully. The rule (rather than the exception) is that a complete restoration is often needed to return it to pristine condition. Because of their higher production totals, there tend to be more "missing for many years" '68 Shelbys than other years. (Photo Courtesy Mike Hudock)

price region. The unfortunate by-product of this value escalation is that it now becomes more worthwhile to put forth the effort to fake a car. When values were lower, creating a Shelby from scratch simply wasn't economically viable. Sadly, now it is.

SHELBY'S MUSTANG, REDEFINED

As with any automobile marque that has been in existence for multiple model years, parking one year's example alongside the next, in chronological order, reveals an evolution in the design and overall character of that marque. The Shelby Mustang family is no exception. In this context, the '68 Shelby Cobra GT occupies what has often been thought of as falling exactly halfway between pure performance and total luxury. In reality, however, it is perhaps better to describe the '68 Shelbys as being just on the luxury side of that hypothetical tipping point; there seems to be more luxury than performance in these cars.

From the GT350's inception in 1965 to the 1968 edition of the same automobile, there is a marked softening of the car's rough-and-ready character as Shelby American (and later Shelby Automotive) expanded the car's consumer base with an increased emphasis on luxury. The 1968 Shelby Cobra GT is clearly not in the same league as that very first GT350 but, rather, in its own league.

Carroll Shelby was all about sports cars. His dream of building an American sports car was realized in 1962 when, with Ford support, he created the Shelby Cobra. In 1965, he accepted the challenge of turning Ford's new, sporty sedan into a legitimate sports car, which he did with the creation of the Mustang GT350. Just a couple of years later, however, he disliked the kind of vehicles that were more than a quarter-ton heavier than that first GT350, but that consumer demand (and the Ford Motor Company) pushed him to create. He felt that they were no longer sports cars.

The advent of the GT500 in 1967 was a big step toward establishing his GT cars as a new class of vehicle. The 1968 Shelby Cobra GT500 KR solidified his Mustang-based Cobra as the true embodiment of what Webster defined as "any of a group of American-made two-door sports coupes with large, powerful engines designed for high-performance driving": the American muscle car.

After only a half-model-year reign, Shelby's muscle Mustang, the King of the Road, was dethroned, but the deposition, although lengthy, didn't last forever. In 2008 and 2009, Shelby Automobiles produced 1,571 twin-nostril retro-hooded GT500 KRs based on Ford's 500-hp Shelby GT500 for the U.S. market (plus a couple hundred more worldwide). The U.S. production quantity mirrored the original KR build total. The new King's 1968-inspired hood was secured by the same type of ACSCO twist locks as the original edition.

COMPARATIVE 1968 SHELBY COBRA PERFORMANCE DATA*

The following data was extracted from the vehicle owner's manual wherever possible.

Vehicle Characteristics	GT350	GT500	GT500 KR
Curb Weight (pounds)	3,146	3,445	3,445
Weight Distribution (percent, front/rear)	53/47	56.4/43.6	56.4/43.6
Wheelbase (inches)	108	108	108
Front Track (inches)	58.1	58.1	58.1
Rear Track (inches)	58.1	58.1	58.1
Length (overall, inches)	186.8	186.8	186.8
Width (overall, inches)	70.9	70.9	70.9
Height (overall, inches)	51.8	51.8	51.8
Body Styles Available	2-door fastback, 2-door convertible	2-door fastback, 2-door convertible	2-door fastback, 2-door convertible
Seating Capacity	4	4	4

Vehicle Performance	GT350	GT500	GT500 KR
0-60 mph (seconds)	6.3	6.5	6.9
0-100 mph (seconds)	17.1	17.1	14.6
Quarter Mile (seconds at MPH)	14.9 at 94	14.8 at 98	14.0 at 103
Top Speed (4th gear, MPH)	119	129	130

Drivetrain	GT350	GT500	GT500 KR
Manual Transmission	Ford Top-loader	Ford Top-loader	Ford Top-loader
Automatic Transmission	Ford C-4	Ford C-6	Ford C-6
Standard Rear-End Ratio	3.89 Manual Trans, 3.50 Auto Trans	3.50 Manual Trans, 3.25 Auto Trans	3.50 Manual Trans, 3.25 Auto Trans
Optional Rear-End Ratios	4.11, 4.56[†]	3.00, 3.25, 4.11, 4.56[†]	3.00, 3.25, 4.11, 4.56[†]

Standard Engines			
Displacement (ci)	302	428	428 Cobra Jet
Bore x Stroke (inches)	4.00 x 3.00	4.13 x 3.984	4.13 x 3.984
Horsepower at RPM	250 at 4,800	360 at 5,400	335 at 5,200
Torque (ft-lbs at RPM)	310 at 2,800	459 at 3,200	440 at 3,400
Compression Ratio	10.5:1	10.5:1	10.6:1
Carburetion	Holley 600-cfm[**], aluminum Cobra intake	Holley 715-cfm[***], aluminum Ford PI intake	Holley 735-cfm, cast-iron Ford intake

* Data for fastback and convertible models similar. ** Early GT350s used Autolite 4100 600-cfm carburetor and Ford cast-iron intake until Holley/Cobra intakes emissions certified. *** A few early GT500s built in January and February 1968 used Autolite 4100 600-cfm carburetor. [†] Extra-cost option.

PRODUCTION NUMBERS, COLORS AND PRICES

Production Numbers

GT350	% of GT350
1,053 fastback	72.2
404 convertible	27.8
4-speed transmission	51.0
Automatic transmission	49.0
Air conditioned	29.7
Non-air conditioned	70.3
Total GT350 production: 1,457; 32.7% of all cars	

GT500	% of GT500
1,020 fastback	71.7
402 convertible	28.3
4-speed transmission	39.2
Automatic transmission	60.8
Air conditioned	29.5
Non-air conditioned	70.5
Total GT500 production: 1,422; 31.9% of all cars	

GT500 KR	% of GT500 KR
1,053 fastback	67.0
518 convertible	33.0
4-speed transmission	50.7
Automatic transmission	48.3
Air conditioned	28.6
Non-air conditioned	71.4
Total GT500 KR production: 1,571; 35.3% of all cars	

Convertible Top	% of Total Build
Black	32.6
Parchment (white)	67.4

1968 Shelby Cobra	% of All Cars
Fastback	70.2
Convertible	29.8
4-speed transmission	47.2
Automatic transmission	52.8
Air conditioned	29.3
Non-air conditioned	70.7
Total 1968 Shelby Mustang Production: 4,450	

Colors Available

Exterior	% of Total Build
Acapulco Blue	17.1
Highland Green	17.0
Raven Black	5.9
Lime Gold	14.6
Sunlit Gold	8.2
Wimbledon White	14.0
Candy Apple Red	19.4
WT 6066 yellow (143 cars)	3.2
Four cars each were built in WT 7081 green and WT 5107 orange	
Two cars each were built in WT 5014 orange and WT 4017 red	
Three cars each were built in WT 5185 orange	
Three cars were painted Royal Maroon; two Brittany Blue; and one Meadowlark Yellow	

Interior	% of Total Build
Black	85.5
Saddle	14.5
One car was delivered with Ivy Gold interior	

1968 Shelby Production Numbers, Colors and Prices
Appendix B

Prices

Base Model	Retail Price
GT350 fastback	$4,116.62
GT350 convertible	4,238.14
GT500 fastback	4,317.39
GT500 convertible	4,438.91
GT500 KR fastback	4,472.57
GT500 KR convertible	4,594.09

Mandatory Options	Retail Price
Power disc brakes	$64.77
Power steering	84.47
Shoulder harness	50.76*
Fold-Down rear seat	64.78
Tilt-Pop steering wheel	66.14

* Fastback and convertible priced identically

Factory Options	Retail Price
Selectaire air conditioning	$356.10
Tinted glass (mandatory with A/C)	30.25
Cruise-O-Matic transmission	50.08
Push-button AM radio	57.59
AM-FM Multiplex Stereo	170.76
Paxton supercharger	*
427 medium-riser engine	**
Traction-Lok rear	***

* GT350 only; advertised but not actually available from the factory, could be dealer-installed
** GT500; advertised but not actually available
*** No cost data available, standard on non-air conditioned GT500 KRs

Production Differences

GT350 and GT500 (Early Production)

- Approx. first 200 cars had dual serial numbers stamped on fender ID tag
- Some GT350s delivered with cast-iron intake manifolds and Autolite 600-cfm carburetors (until Cobra intake received emissions certification)
- Some early GT500s delivered with Autolite 600-cfm carburetors
- Rectangular rear quarter-panel side marker lights
- Marchal fog lights
- Tilt steering wheel not installed on some cars
- Smooth vinyl seat inserts
- 1967-type Shelby American fender ID tag blanks (and door sill labels)
- White letter Goodyear Speedway 350 E70-15 tires
- Smooth black or Saddle upholstery

GT350 and GT500 (Later Production)

- GT350s had COBRA aluminum intake with Holley carburetor
- Single serial number in fender ID tag
- Pointed rear quarter-panel side marker lights
- Shelby Automotive fender ID tag and door sill labels
- Door ID tag carried the wording "Special Performance Vehicle"
- Tilt-Pop steering wheel became a standard Shelby feature
- Lucas fog lights
- Slight differences exist in the shape of the lower body scoops, likely due to a mold change; not generally correlated to "early" or "late" cars
- Blackwall Goodyear Polyglas E70-15 tires
- Smooth Saddle or Comfort Weave black upholstery

GT500 KR

- Single serial number in fender ID tag
- Pointed rear quarter-panel side marker lights
- "Shelby Automotive" fender ID tag and door sill labels
- Door ID tag carried the wording "Special Performance Vehicle"
- Tilt-Pop steering wheel
- Lucas fog lights
- Ram air plenum added to underside of hood
- GT500 KR side stripe, "428 Cobra Jet" fender badge and "Cobra Jet" dash badge, fuel
- cap and wheel cover center caps
- Blackwall Goodyear Polyglas E70-15 tires
- Cobra Jet (larger diameter) exhaust system with four-pipe exhaust tips
- Electronic starter delay module
- Staggered rear shocks (manual transmission cars only)
- Wood/silver inlaid automatic transmission shift handle
- Additional sheet steel wrap to lower front shock towers
- Autolite non-adjustable rear shocks (manual transmission cars only)
- Smooth Saddle or Comfort Weave black upholstery

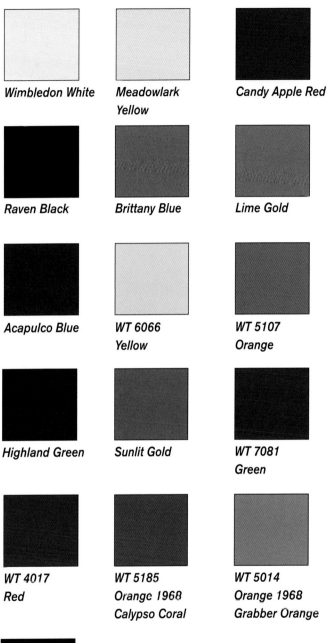

1968 Shelby Cobra Color Chips

Wimbledon White	*Meadowlark Yellow*	*Candy Apple Red*
Raven Black	*Brittany Blue*	*Lime Gold*
Acapulco Blue	*WT 6066 Yellow*	*WT 5107 Orange*
Highland Green	*Sunlit Gold*	*WT 7081 Green*
WT 4017 Red	*WT 5185 Orange 1968 Calypso Coral*	*WT 5014 Orange 1968 Grabber Orange*

Royal Maroon

1968 SHELBY NUMEROLOGY: VIN CODES AND TAGS

Even though the Mustangs shipped to Shelby Automotive (and earlier, to Shelby American) for conversion to GT350s and GT500s were not complete cars, they were well past the point at which they received their Ford Mustang Vehicle Identification Numbers (VINs). In 1965, 1966, and 1967, Shelby American removed the cars' Mustang door identification tags, which contained the Ford VIN, among other construction data such as the car's build date, and obscured the inner fender Ford VIN, covering it with a Shelby American identification tag, which assigned the former Ford Mustang a new Shelby GT350 or GT500 serial number and identity.

The correlation between those first three years' Ford and Shelby VINs is known only to a small group of historians from the Shelby American Automobile Club Registry. They can provide a potential buyer of one of these automobiles with some manner of assurance that the Shelby they want to add to their collection appears to be constructed on the correct Ford Mustang platform. This is important, as the desirability and the values of these cars continue to escalate well past 30 times their original sticker price.

Although the 1968 Shelbys still concealed the Mustang's original Ford inner fender VIN with a Shelby ID tag, that tag contained the car's original Ford VIN. In addition, the retention of the Ford Mustang door data plate as well as the addition of a Ford VIN windshield tag gave the '68 Shelby several visible Ford VINs as well as its corresponding Shelby VIN; the correlation between the Ford and Shelby VINs are no longer secret.

Following is an explanation of the identification tags visible on any given '68 Shelby Cobra.

Fender ID Tag

An early incarnation of the vehicle numbering scheme incorporated both the Mustang's original Ford VIN and a unique Shelby Automotive VIN number on the Shelby serial number tag, under which lies the

stamped Ford VIN. With this scheme, the Mustang number appeared on the upper portion of the serial plate and the Shelby number below. This dual numbering scheme was used on approximately the first 200 cars.

An example of the early dual serial numbering scheme on a Ford Mustang is:

8T03S116062/SHELBY 8D410C22A00250

Ford Mustang VIN (upper number)

8 = 1968 model year
T = Metuchen Assembly Plant
03 = Body style (02: fastback, 03: convertible)
S = Engine (J: 302/GT350, R: 428 Cobra Jet/GT500 KR*, S: 428/GT500)
116062 = Consecutive Ford production number (Mustangs began with 100001 each model year)

Dual serial number usage discontinued before GT500 KR production began, thus, there are no dual serial number GT500 KRs ("R" code engine).

Shelby VIN (lower number)

8 = 1968 model year
D = Type of order (D = domestic, X = export)
4 = Engine (2: 302/GT350, 3: Paxton supercharged [assigned but never implemented], 4: 428/GT500, 5: 427/GT500 [assigned but never implemented])
1 = Transmission (0: 4-speed, 1: automatic)

0 = Air conditioning (0: no A/C, 1: A/C)
C = Body style (C: convertible, F: fastback)
2 = Exterior color (1: Sunlit Gold, 2: Acapulco Blue, 3: Raven Black, 4: Wimbledon White, 5: Highland Green, 6: Candy Apple Red, 7: Lime Gold); Shelby used a unique numbering series for the colors different from Ford color codes
2 = Convertible top color (1: black top/glass rear window, 2: Parchment [white] top/glass rear window, 0: fastback, no convertible top)
A = Interior color (A: black, D: Saddle)
00250 = Consecutive Shelby production number

It was soon recognized that there was a certain degree of redundancy in the two (Ford and Shelby) VINs (as well as the door data plate) so the unique Shelby VIN was eventually dropped and the vehicle's "official" VIN became the Ford VIN with the consecutive Shelby production number added to the end following a "-". This is sometimes referred to as the "combined" (or "simplified") serial number and was used for the majority of '68 Shelby production.

Both the dual and combined serial numbers, for quite a while, used VIN tag blanks that were nearly identical to the 1967 style of serial plate. It has often been believed that they were, in fact, unused 1967 serial tags. Closer examination of these 1968 tags, however, reveals that the text line "Los Angeles, Calif." is missing from under the "Shelby American" nomenclature of the 1967 style of tag. This confirms that although the 1967 artwork may have been used for a run of 1968 serial tags, that artwork was modified to delete the former California place of manufacture and the tags are not 1967 "leftovers."

Later '68 Shelbys carried serial tags with the more correct "Shelby Automotive" nomenclature. Door sill labels essentially mirrored the serial tag usage. Cars with "Shelby American" serial tags used "Shelby American Los Angeles, California" door sill labels but when the serial tags were switched to the "Shelby Automotive" style, "Shelby Automotive" door sill labels came into use.

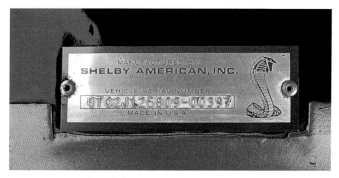

An example of the later, combined numbering system (with Ford and Shelby numbers combined, Shelby American tag) is:

8T02J126809-00397

8T02J126809 = same as above example
00397 = Consecutive Shelby production number (0001 through 04450)

1968 Shelby Numerology: VIN Codes and Tags
Appendix C

Windshield Identification Tag

A small identification tag stamped with the Mustang's (actually, all 1968 Ford vehicles) Ford VIN is riveted to the top of the dash so that it is visible through the windshield on the passenger's side. This allowed the vehicle's Ford VIN to be read without having to open the driver's door or the hood.

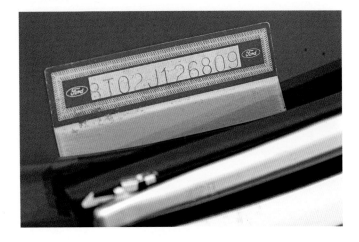

Door Warranty Identification Tag

1968 was the first year that Shelby Mustangs retained their Ford warranty identification tag on the edge of the driver's door. Information contained on the aluminum tag consists of the following:

- 8T02J126809 = Ford VIN (explained above)
- Body = 63B (fastback, Interior Décor Group); 76B (convertible, Interior Décor Group)
- Color = D: Acapulco Blue; Y: Sunlit Gold; A: Raven Black; M: Wimbledon White; R: Highland Green; T: Candy Apple Red; I: Lime Gold; B: Royal Maroon; Q: Brittany Blue; W: Meadowlark Yellow; blank: special "WT" colors. With the exception of the special "WT" colors, codes used were standard Ford color codes.
- Trim = 5A (Comfort Weave Charcoal Black Interior Décor bucket seats); 6A (Charcoal Black Interior Décor bucket seats); 6F (Medium Saddle Interior Décor bucket seats). Trim variation indicated by second "A" ("6FA"); no Comfort Weave convertibles or Saddle
- Date = Vehicle final assembly date 11M (December 11 (1967))
- DSO = 8D2553: 8D denotes the district where Mustangs destined for Shelby Automotive were built; 2553 indicates the DSO (batch) from which this particular Mustang originated
- Axle = 1: 3.89; 6: 3.00; 7: 3.00 Traction-Lok; 8: 3.50; H: 3.50 Traction-Lok (Due to space constraints on the tag, the district, DSO, and axle are strung together and appear as a single number). Note that Shelby used a unique set of axle codes different from Mustangs and other standard Ford vehicles.
- Trans = 5: 4-speed wide-ratio manual; W: C-4 automatic; U: C-6 automatic

A later version of the door tag was identical to the earlier type except for the "Special Performance Vehicle" warning (which translates to "limited warranty").

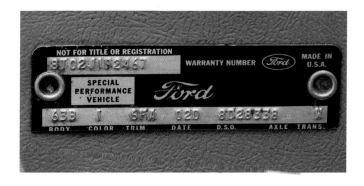

Body Buck Tag

The "buck" is the beginning of a car's unibody chassis. The "body buck tag" is screwed to the passenger-side inner fender in the vicinity of the shock absorber "beehive." Its purpose is to ensure proper sequencing of the installation of a vehicle's options. Although all Mustang assembly plants eventually used buck tags, the '68 Shelby was the first to carry them. This is because Shelby's former source of Mustangs, the San Jose assembly plant, didn't use buck tags until 1970. Metuchen used them from the start of its Mustang production in early 1965. Information contained on the buck tag consists of the following:

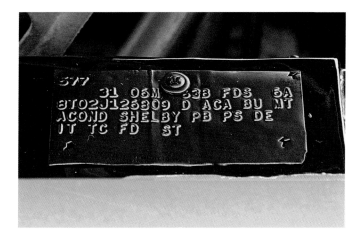

- First line: 577 (internal production sequence number).
- Second line: 11 (buck assembly slot number); 05M = buck assembly date (December 5 [1967]); 63B =

(fastback, Interior Décor Group); FDS = Fold Down Seat; 6A = (Charcoal Black Interior Décor bucket seat). Other interior options were 5A (Charcoal Black Knitted (Comfort Weave), Interior Décor bucket seat), or 6F (Medium Saddle Interior Décor bucket seat).

- Third Line: 8T02J126809 = Ford VIN (explained above); D ACA BU MET = Color Code D, Acapulco Blue Metallic (standard Ford color codes used). Metallic color sometimes also annotated as "MT."
- Fourth Line: ACOND = Air Conditioning; SHFLBY = Mustang built for Shelby conversion; PB = Power Brakes; PS = Power Steering; DE = Dual Exhaust. Air Conditioning also sometimes annotated as "AC."
- Fifth Line: IT = Interior Trim Package; TC = Tilt-Away Steering Column; FD = Fold Down Seat (repeated on second line as "FDS"); ST = Standard Transmission.

The annotation for Mustangs destined for conversion to Shelby GT350s and GT500s was changed to "SA" on later tags. In an effort to recoup some financial losses from the September-November 1967 UAW strike, rear bumperettes became an extra-cost option in calendar year 1968 and were annotated on the buck tags as "RB." AM/FM radio was annotated by either "STEREO" or "LP."

Only two choices for convertible tops were available on Shelbys and they were noted as "TOP2" (for Black power top with glass rear window) or "TOP4" (for Parchment power top with glass rear window). Both were changed to simply "PT" later in the year. The unusually shaped holes in the buck tags are inspector's stampings, punched as the car passed through several in-process inspection points.

Shelbys painted any of the special "WT" colors had the color block in the door tag blank. The Ford color number was also omitted from the third line of the buck tag, but the special color number (WT 7081, green in these examples, courtesy of Mike Tillery) appeared on the lower line of the buck tag.

1968 Shelby Mustang GT350, GT500 and GT500KR
In Detail No. 3

The first-year GT350 was pure performance to almost
the complete exhaustion of all other attributes. The 1968
Shelby Cobra showcased distinctive styling with luxury and
comfort features over performance, but not to the complete
abandonment of it.

MUSCLE CARS
IN DETAIL

Each volume in the all-new In Detail series from CarTech provides an incredible amount of detail on a single model of iconic muscle car, all at a very affordable price. Included is an introduction and historical overview, an explanation of the design and concepts involved in creating the car, a look at marketing and promotion, and an in-depth study of all hardware and available options, as well as an examination of where the car is on the market today. Also included is an appendix of paint and option codes, VIN and build-tag decoders, as well as production numbers

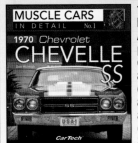

1970 CHEVROLET CHEVELLE SS: In Detail No. 1 by Dale McIntosh

As with all In Detail Series titles, this book provides an introduction and historical overview, an explanation of the design and concepts involved in creating the car, a look at marketing and promotion, and an in-depth study of all hardware and available options, as well as an examination of where the 1970 Chevelle SS is in the market today. 8.25 x 9", 96 pgs, 110 photos. Sftbd. Part # CT588........................ **$18.95**

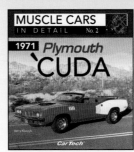

1971 PLYMOUTH 'CUDA: IN DETAIL NO. 2 by Ola Nilsson

This volume provides an introduction and historical overview, an explanation of the design and concepts involved in creating the car, a look at marketing and promotion, an in-depth study of all hardware and available options, as well as an examination of where the car is on the market today. 8.25 x 9", 96 pgs, 110 photos. Sftbd. Part # CT576........ **$18.95**

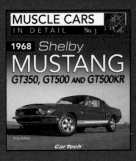

Muscle Cars In Detail #3
1968 Shelby Mustang GT350, GT500 and GT500KR

By Greg Kolasa

Now that you are the proud owner of this book, check out all the other titles in this exciting series.

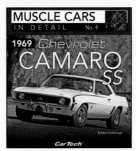

1969 CHEVROLET CAMARO SS: In Detail No. 4 by Robert Kimbrough

This Volume No. 4 of CarTech's In Detail series provides an introduction and historical overview, an explanation of the design and concepts involved in creating the 1969 Camaro SS, a look at marketing and promotion, an in-depth study of all hardware and available options, as well as an examination of where the car is on the market today. 8.25 x 9", 96 pgs, 110 photos, Sftbd. Part # CT564 .... **$18.95**

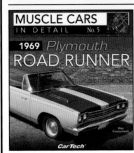

1969 PLYMOUTH ROAD RUNNER: In Detail No. 5 by Wes Eisenschenk

This Volume No. 5 of CarTech's In Detail series provides an introduction and historical overview, an explanation of the design and concepts involved in creating the 1969 Road Runner, a look at marketing and promotion, an in-depth study of all hardware and available options, as well as an examination of where the car is on the market today. 8.25 x 9", 96 pgs, 120 photos, Sftbd. Part # CT580 .... **$18.95**

1973–1974 PONTIAC TRANS-AM SUPER DUTY 455: In Detail No. 6 by Barry Klyczyk

This Volume No. 6 of CarTech's In Detail series provides an introduction and historical overview, an explanation of the design and concepts involved in creating the Trans-Am Super Duty, a look at marketing and promotion, an in-depth study of all hardware and available options, as well as an examination of where the car is on the market today. 8.25 x 9", 96 pgs, 110 photos, Sftbd. Part # CT583 ....**$18.95**